THIS *Cinderella* HAS BIG FEET

Ditching perfect for a beautifully imperfect life

LYNETTE BEELER

Special Thanks

I'd like to express a special thank you to all of my friends and family who have inspired me throughout this process with your prayers, support, and many words of inspiration. I couldn't have completed this without you.

My incredible husband, thank you for your continued encouragement that has provoked me throughout this season. Thank you, babe, for being my biggest fan and loving me enough to not let me quit. I love and honor you!

To my beautiful daughters, many of the lessons I've learned and am sharing throughout this book are because of you. God gave me three precious gifts who in your own unique ways have sharpened me. Thank you for your support and input in this work. You've been used by God to make me a better woman. I love you!

Lastly, but most importantly, I want to thank my Heavenly Father who has been so patient and gracious with me. I've been

THIS CINDERELLA HAS BIG FEET

a tough nut to crack, but I'm so grateful You never gave up on me. I pray this book is a testimony that will honor You and show others what a wonderful Father You truly are!

Copyright © 2025 by Lynette Beeler

All rights reserved.

ISBN: 979-8-9988812-0-6

No portion of this book may be reproduced in any form without written permission from the author, except as permitted by U.S. copyright law.

All scriptures used are taken from the Holy Bible.
Scripture quotations marked NLT are taken from the Holy Bible, New Living Translation. Copyright © 1996, 2004, 2015 by Tyndale House Foundation. Used by permission of Tyndale House Ministries, Carol Stream, Illinois 60188. All rights reserved.
Scripture quotations marked NIV are taken from the Holy Bible, New International Version®, NIV®. Copyright © 1973, 1978, 1984, 2011 by Biblica, Inc.® Used by permission of Zondervan. All rights reserved worldwide. www.zondervan.com. The "NIV" and "New International Version" are trademarks registered in the United States Patent and Trademark Office by Biblica, Inc.®
Scripture quotations marked ESV are taken from the ESV® Bible (The Holy Bible, English Standard Version®). Copyright © 2001 by Crossway, a publishing ministry of Good News Publishers. Used by permission. All rights reserved.
Scripture quotations marked KJV are taken from the King James Version. Public domain.
Scripture quotations marked NKJV are taken from the New King James Version®. Copyright © 1982 by Thomas Nelson. Used by permission. All rights reserved.
Scripture quotations marked MSG are taken from THE MESSAGE. Copyright © 1993, 2002, 2018 by Eugene H. Peterson. Used by permission of NavPress. All rights reserved. Represented by Tyndale House Publishers, a Division of Tyndale House Ministries.
Scripture quotations marked NASB are taken from the New American Standard Bible® (NASB). Copyright © 1960, 1962, 1963, 1968, 1971, 1972, 1973, 1975, 1977, 1995 by The Lockman Foundation. Used by permission. www.Lockman.org.
Scripture quotations marked TPT are from The Passion Translation®. Copyright © 2017, 2018, 2020 by Passion & Fire Ministries, Inc. Used by permission. All rights reserved. ThePassionTranslation.com.

THIS CINDERELLA HAS BIG FEET

Scripture quotations marked BSB are taken from the Berean Standard Bible, BSB is produced in cooperation with Bible Hub, Discovery Bible, OpenBible.com, and the Berean Bible Translation Committee. This text of God's Word has been dedicated to the public domain.

Scripture quotations taken from the Amplified® Bible (AMP), Copyright © 2015 by The Lockman Foundation. Used by permission. lockman.org.

Contents

Introduction	1
1. Worth It	5
2. No Negotiating	15
3. Performing for Acceptance	23
4. Not Perfect but Perfecting	31
5. Fear Isn't Fair	39
6. No More Hiding	51
7. I Need Some Grace	63
8. Invited But Not Really	71
9. Better Broken	81
10. A Little Margin Goes A Long Way	95
11. Contentment in the Most Unlikely Place	107
12. Acceptance and Trust	117
13. Sisters Are Necessary	127
14. Now A Princess	139
To the reader	147

Introduction

"Not that I have already obtained this or am already perfect, but I press on to make it my own, because Christ has made me his own" (Philippians 3:12, ESV).

It was a beautiful Saturday morning. Spring had finally sprung in Michigan one week before Easter. My tradition of buying Easter dresses and shoes for my girls had not yet happened but the day's weather was ideal for a little shopping trip. We piled the girls into the van and drove to several stores to find the perfect outfits for my little princesses.

After finding their dresses, we proceeded to another store with shoes displayed wall to wall for every occasion, and sure enough, we found shoes for each of them – just one problem – my oldest was having a meltdown. The pretty pink shoes I found to match her dress became a small crisis once she tried them on. She let me know they were just too tight! The shoes that looked perfect in the box were painful on her feet!

I wish this experience would have spoken to me then like it does now. There are so many things in this life that we imagine will be perfect only to find that they are not. Metaphorically speaking, we can force our feet into some beautiful shoes that do not fit trying to produce the perfect ensemble. In doing so we set ourselves up to suffer the painful consequences caused by bunions later.

I will be the first to admit that the lessons I have learned have often come the hard way, by experience! Instead of listening and learning from other people's mistakes, I chose to make them myself. The process of living and learning has caused many painful results that could have been avoided had I chose to apply the knowledge good people throughout my life have shared with me. Knowledge is knowing that something is true, but wisdom is applying that truth in our lives.

As my dad used to say, *"Lessons are better caught than taught."* It is my hope that this book will serve as a resource to offer some valuable insights that will help you catch the truth of some lessons already learned rather than having to be taught through repeated mistakes. I pray it will shed the light of truth over the darkness of any and every lie that you may have unknowingly believed. It is my desire to help you avoid the discomfort associated with trying to fit into roles that are unsuitable, wasting precious time striving for outcomes that are more of a fantasy than reality.

Each chapter is written with candor as I share different stories and lessons I've learned throughout my journey. Many times, these lessons were taught through adversity that I brought on myself. I tried in vain to wear God's shoes of control, endeavoring to manipulate a perfect outcome based on unrealistic expectations. One big lesson I've learned through the pain is that life will never be perfect, but it can still be beautiful!

P.S. Each chapter ends with a prayer, inviting you to take a moment to reflect and pray. Every prayer is tailored to the chapter and provides a simple way to connect personally with your Heavenly Father. After praying, I want to encourage you to pause and listen for any specific guidance or prompting you might receive from Him as He responds.

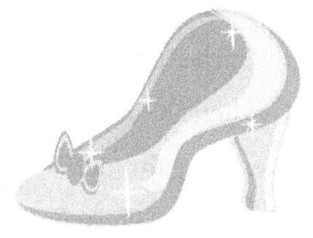

Chapter 1

Worth It

"There will always be someone who can't see your worth. Don't let it be you." ~ Mel Robbins

I'm a huge fan of shopping; I'd call it a hobby, but I'm sure it doesn't qualify as such. My approach to shopping may be drastically different than what you're thinking, because I love to shop but hate to spend money. It seems like an oxymoron, an impossible combination, doesn't it? Well, it's not! Often, the thrill is in looking for the next BIG deal! It's exhilarating to find an item priced well below its value. Through the years, thrifting has been a fun experience because I can usually find valuable items for a fraction of the price that I would have paid in a department store. One such purchase was a brand-new carpet cleaning machine, still in the box. It was less than half the price I would have paid elsewhere. Spotting a deal with or without a follow-up purchase is exciting for me.

I've had many occasions where my finds have been amazing! Well, at least I thought they were, but my husband, not so much. I remember a specific hunt I went on was for a purse. I had always wanted a Coach purse, but the thought of paying their ticketed price seemed ridiculous to me. So, I made it my mission to find the perfect Coach purse within my pennies budget. My shopping led me to an online store with deals beaming from page to page. In my mind, I had hit the jackpot! I finally narrowed my search to a medium-sized bag that combined several colors I was sure would match any outfit in my wardrobe. The day came when my purse finally arrived. With much anticipation, I tore open the package to reveal what I thought to be a Coach purse was merely a cheap imitation of one. The thrill I once had was replaced with frustration and regret. Can you relate? Have you ever purchased an item with great expectation of what that item would look like or do for you, but you were met with great disappointment in its performance?

I used to think the Lord thought that about me. I grew up in church and heard the following scripture, "Don't you realize that your body is the temple of the Holy Spirit, who lives in you and was given to you by God? You are not your own for God bought you with a high price. So, you must glorify God with your body" (I Corinthians 6:19-20, NLT). Understanding the high price Jesus Christ paid for my salvation, I was sure He had buyer's remorse when looking at me! I have spent much of my life trying to become "good enough" for His amazing love and live up to this high value. I wore myself out with activities I felt necessary to gain His approval and earn His love, but I also worked equally hard to gain people's approval and affection.

At the young age of 25, I stepped into the pastorate of a church that had only ever had one pastor and a wife that could do everything. She was good at speaking, decorating, singing, playing piano, running large conferences, directing community Bible studies, spearheading new ministries, and more. I felt so small and insignificant stepping in to take her place. I couldn't preach, play piano, or spearhead any conference; I could barely sing with any amount of confidence. The shoes that were once wore by the "perfect" pastor's wife, in my eyes, were now lying at my doorstep, and they just didn't fit! I tried so hard to wear them, all the while feeling miserable and less and less adequate.

My husband tried hard to encourage me and pull me out of my shell. He would say, "Babe, I think you could do a great job speaking to the women; how about speaking on Mother's Day?" That sounds like a real compliment, doesn't it? But, through my filter of insecurity, what I heard was, "You're not doing enough;

you need to step up and do more! You're just not good enough!" Oh, how the enemy of our soul manipulates the truth, and the sad reality is that I believed his lies.

> *The thoughts of inadequacy screaming, "You're not good enough," can bombard us daily. If it's not performance-based, it hits us at the core of our beauty, intelligence, or relationships.*

We scrutinize ourselves with a critical eye based on the negative words and opinions of others and our own negative thinking. With the media culture around us, we cannot escape the constant messaging telling us we're not enough! We need to do more, be more, and get more to be happy. The struggle is real, and I've come to realize I am not the only one who has struggled.

This book was born from experiences I have lived and learned on my journey towards wholeness and peace. The striving for perfection has left me scarred but not defeated. My scars tell a story of hope and redemption found in Jesus Christ. Through sharing a few stories with you, my prayer is that it will help you avoid unnecessary pain and overcome any areas of insecurity that make you feel as if you need to do more or be more to be valued and loved.

"...For He (God) said, 'Anyone who harms you harms my most precious possession'" (Zechariah 2:8, NLT).

Another translation states that anyone who touches you touches the apple of His eye. He's talking about you. You are His valuable possession; His VALUABLE POSSESSION is you! The amazing thing is that God did not make this statement in Zechariah to a bunch of perfect kids doing everything right. He made this statement about His kids who were being selfish, rebellious, and downright unlovable, yet God was unmoved in His love for them.

When I understood the context of whom God was saying this to, it shifted something in me. I began to understand God's love for me is not based on me; it's simply placed on me. He paid a price that was so great it forced a high value on me. I'm literally priceless and so are you. There's no other human just like you or me; we are a one-of-a-kind masterpiece.

> *Just like "beauty is in the eye of the beholder," so is the value set by the purchaser. No one pays a high price for something unless they think it's worth it.*

If Jesus didn't think you were worth it, He wouldn't have paid such a high price for you! He didn't go online looking for a bargain, only to end up with an imitation of someone else. He paid the ultimate price for the authentic, original version of you because you are worth it!

I want to share some insights from God's word that I hope will help you see yourself from His perspective and grasp the magnitude of His great love for you. Understanding His love is essential for moving beyond our faults and failures to embrace the freedom He offers.

"And you will know the truth and the truth will set you free" (John 8:32, NLT).

The only thing that breaks the back of deception is truth! To know who God says we are, we must first understand who He is. Once we understand who He is, the utterance of His spoken name carries the proper weight of significance. ~John Piper

There are words that have been spoken over us by people we love, words spoken over us by our culture, and words spoken over us by ourselves. It's time to break free from toxic thinking and negative words that we've allowed to define us. We must put a stop to the enemy's voice that would love to delay or destroy our destiny by calling us something we're NOT (weak, failure, ugly, broken, dumb, unwanted, etc.)!

It's time to begin believing and decreeing what God has said about us!

1. We are loved.

"But God shows his love for us in that while we were still sinners, Christ died for us" (Romans 5:8, ESV).

"This is real love—not that we loved God, but that he loved us and sent his Son as a sacrifice to take away our sins" (1 John 4:10, NLT).

2. We are chosen.

"Before I shaped you in the womb, I knew you intimately. I had divine plans for you before I gave you life and set you apart and chose you to be mine…" (Jeremiah 1:5, Passion Translation).
"…You are a chosen people. You are royal priests, a holy nation, God's very own possession. As a result, you can show others the goodness of God, for he called you out of the darkness into his wonderful light" (1 Peter 2:9, NLT).

3. We are free.

"For freedom Christ has set us free; stand firm therefore, and do not submit again to a yoke of slavery" (Galatians 5:1, ESV).
"For the law of the Spirit of life has set you free in Jesus Christ from the law of sin and of death" (Romans 8:2, ESV).

4. We are protected in Christ.

"He who dwells in the shelter of the Most High will abide in the shadow of the Almighty. I will say to the Lord, 'My refuge and my fortress, my God, in You I trust.' For he will deliver you from the snare of the fowler and from the deadly pestilence. He will cover you with his pinions, and under his wings you will find refuge; his faithfulness is a shield and buckler" (Psalms 91:1-4, ESV).

5. We are made new.

"Therefore, if anyone is in Christ, he is a new creation; The old has passed away; behold, the new has come" (2 Corinthians 5:17, ESV).

6. We are an heir to all God has.

"Now, you are no longer a slave, but God's own child; and since you are His child, God has made you His heir" (Galatians 4:7, NLT).

7. We are forgiven.

"If we confess our sins, he is faithful and just to forgive us our sins and to cleanse us from all unrighteousness" (1 John 1:9, ESV).
"He saved us, not because of the righteous things we had done, but because of His mercy. He washed away our sins, giving us a new birth and new life through the Holy Spirit" (Titus 3:5, NLT).

8. We are a child of God.

"But to all who believed Him and accepted Him, He gave the right to become children of God" (John 1:12, NLT).
"And I will be a Father to you, and you will be my sons and daughters, says the Lord Almighty" (2 Corinthians 6:18, NIV).

9. We are provided for.

"And my God will supply every need of yours according to His riches in glory in Christ Jesus" (Philippians 4:19, ESV). "Therefore, I tell you, do not be anxious about your life, what you will eat or what you will drink, nor about your body, what you will put on. Is not life more than food, and the body more than clothing? Look at the birds of the air: they neither sow nor reap nor gather into barns, and yet your heavenly Father feeds them. Are you not of more value than they" (Matthew 6:25-26, ESV)?

10. We have a purpose.

"I know the plans I have for you, says the Lord. They are plans for good and not for disaster, to give you a future and a hope" (Jeremiah 29:11, NLT).

This is truth, but it will be hard to know and understand it as truth without knowing the person of truth, Jesus Christ. He is more than a myth, a good teacher, or a religious figure. He is God Almighty, the Creator of the universe; yet He is so personal and relational and desires a close relationship with you.

If you have begun reading this book but seriously do not understand who the person of Jesus Christ is, His invitation to experience a life filled with love, peace, and purpose is extended to you. Please take a moment to ask Him to reveal it. You can talk to Him just like a friend because He is. You can start a relationship with Him by praying this simple prayer:

Jesus, I need you and ask you to come into my life. Forgive my selfishness and sin. I want to know you and experience your love and life for me. Help me to understand your Word and grow in truth. Thank you for the price you paid for my healing and salvation. Please reveal your purpose for me and give me the grace to walk in it. Amen.

I'm thrilled about your new relationship with our Heavenly Father. We are family now, so as you continue reading, know that I'm with you every step of the way, praying and cheering you on. I believe that great things will evolve in your life as you grow in your understanding and knowledge of Truth. Let me encourage you to do two things in this new adventure:

1. Tell someone about your decision to know and follow Jesus.
2. Find a church community that will support you in your walk of faith and help you understand the depth of the Father's love for you.

Now, let's continue this journey together.

Chapter 2

No Negotiating

"If you don't know your own value, somebody will tell you your value, and it'll be less than you're worth." ~ Bernard Hopkins

    As I shared in the previous chapter, I like to shop, and I'm pretty good at finding items to purchase for less than they're worth. I can hardly contain my excitement when I stumble across a really good sale. I remember a shopping trip when I spotted a beautiful green jacket. I adored this little beauty, but the coat was not on sale. Being the thrift-minded shopper that I am, I decided to wait for a sale to purchase it. A few weeks later, I returned to the store to see if the coat was still available. When

I arrived, I was concerned that there was only one left in my size. The listed sale price was still not within my budget, but I tried it on anyways. It was then that I noticed a slight flaw. Someone had mistakenly marked on the coat sleeve with a black pen. Oh no, I thought, then, oh yes!! With a mark on the sleeve, I took it to the register to see what the cashier could do. To my surprise, she told me the sale price was less than what was listed, and she took an additional percentage off, so I bought it!

The bargaining begins ...

This is what Satan does in our lives. He magnifies our flaws and makes us believe our value is less because of it. He tries hard to negotiate a price we will settle for that is far below our worth, but his bargaining is never fair. We cannot drop our price based on his appraisal. He will always magnify our weaknesses while minimizing our strengths. You must remember that "God bought you with a high price" (1 Corinthians 6:20a, NLT). Therefore, your value has already been set by the high price Jesus has already paid.

Unlike the coat I bought, your flaws may actually enhance and add value to your life. Let me explain:
In 1918, the United States Postal Service issued a two color 24 cent stamp with a picture of the JN-4 (Jenny) airplane flying on it. The only problem is that the airplane was flying upside down. 700 stamps were produced in sheets of 100 before the U.S. Postal

Service caught the error. Six sheets were destroyed but one was sold to a stamp collector, later this sheet of rare stamps was separated and sold individually. In 2007, one of these rare stamps sold at an auction for a whopping $977,500. The flaw caused this $.24 stamp to escalate in price to almost a million dollars. Later the post office re-released this stamp of the upside-down flying airplane but as you can imagine the duplicates were never as valuable as the originals.

The same is true of you. You are the original, one of a kind, you. No one else is meant to duplicate your design. Your face, body, intellect, and talents are all specific to you. Unfortunately, we live in a lucid culture of transition and duplicates. Instead of cultivating the gifts in our own unique lives, we seek to emulate others. Over-exposure to the highlight reels of others can fan the flames of discontentment in our own lives. Take a step back and ask yourself, "Have I been trying to duplicate the gifts of others in my life?" Though, in theory, this may seem like a good thing, it can have a negative effect if we lose sight of our own creativity and originality. For years, this plagued me, and if not for the grace of God, it would have taken me out of ministry altogether.

"...But when they measure themselves by one another and compare themselves with one another, they are without understanding" (2 Corinthians 10:12, ESV).

As I shared earlier, I stepped into being a senior pastor's wife at the ripe age of 25 with absolutely no experience. I didn't have a clue what the actual "job description" was or what was expected of me. I assumed that what I needed to do was what other pastor's wives did. To say the least, I felt incredibly inadequate in this new position. So, I worked hard to cultivate in me the gifts I saw in others. Unfortunately, many of their gifts were just not my gifts no matter how hard I tried. The harder I tried the more insecure and frustrated I felt. I was losing myself in a world of duplicity that I had manufactured.

I grew up as a PK (preacher's kid) with a Wonder Woman mom who was great at hospitality. She was always opening our home for people to come and stay. I do not remember many times in my life when we didn't have at least one person (who was not family) living with us. She was a great cook and hostess that excelled at making people feel welcome. I, on the other hand, loathed cooking! It was a chore I knew needed to be done as a wife and mother, but it was NOT enjoyable. There was little passion that filled me as I served in this capacity. I just didn't understand why I couldn't replicate this life of hospitality and have the same joy and pleasure my mom did.

It wasn't until years later that I discovered this just wasn't my gift and I didn't have to feel bad about it. My wiring and gifting's were different. I'm an introvert by nature, and though I love being with people, I am often drained by exposure. It takes me pulling away to a quiet place to recharge. I didn't understand this part of me so I'd often feel bad when my husband, who is an extrovert, would spontaneously invite people over to the house or make plans to go out. I'd feel tension and anxiety with an unplanned encounter with others.

I thought there was something wrong with me. Often, I'd cry and ask God to help me, even change me. There were also times I'd get mad and didn't know why. "Why, Lord, do I feel this frustration? Why can't I be like my mom? It would make things so much easier." God did respond, but not how I expected. Instead of changing my wiring, He began to show me that the grace He put on my life was different than my mom's, and He was okay with that. Was I? He patiently waited for me to recognize it and begin to run confidently with the unique gifts He had given ME.

I wasted many of my early years as a wife, mother, ministry partner, and friend trying to be something I was not. I used my energy pursuing the approval of God and people by doing things I just wasn't wired to do. Once I finally came to grips with the reality that God didn't expect me to be a duplicate of anyone else, but his own, unique daughter, life and ministry took on a whole new purpose, fulfillment and passion.

Maybe you can't relate to my story of ministry, but maybe you can relate to trying to compete or measure up to a neighbor, co-worker, sibling, or another person in your life. Your gaze has settled in on the strengths and gifts you see in them, all the while magnifying the discrepancies you see in yourself. Your love for life has been squashed by the ever-increasing pressure to fit in, measure up or flat out over-achieve, thinking, just maybe, it will be the key to your happiness and acceptance in life.

Oh, what a gerbil's wheel that is! It will keep you running but never progressing and never satisfied! You must understand and embrace the fact that you are made to be different. Your worth is in the originality of your creativity and design. It's time to embrace it. Stop beating yourself up for who you're not and rest in the grace of God for who you are. It's your key to healthy contentment that will allow you to enjoy your life again.

> *You're a masterpiece exclusively made by your Creator; what you have perceived as a flaw may actually be something He has intentionally allowed in your life to produce what He saw this world needed from you.*

I think of the Apostle Paul, who was given a thorn in the flesh (2 Corinthians 12:7-9). No one has been able to disclose what the thorn was, but many have speculated it could have been a physical ailment that kept Paul ever aware of his weakness and need for Christ. It is also what kept him from boasting and being arrogant. Sometimes that's exactly why the Lord allows what we perceive as a weakness to be present in our lives. The flaw makes us aware of our need for Christ. It may also be what the Lord uses to keep us compassionate, humble, and relatable to others who need what we have to share.

Let me conclude by saying, we all have the ability to learn, grow, and expand our gifts. This chapter is not meant to discourage growth. The problem is when we try to develop something in us that we think will make us more worthy, liked, or fulfilled based on other people's opinions rather than our Creator's. If the Lord has given you grace for it, go for it! If not, stop wasting precious time and invest in being the best version of you to the world around you for the glory of God!

Lie: I must be more like ... to be valuable.
Truth:

"What sorrow awaits those who argue with their Creator. Does a clay pot argue with its maker? Does the clay dispute with the one who shapes it, saying, 'Stop, you're doing it wrong!' Does the pot exclaim, 'How clumsy can you be?' How terrible it would be if a newborn baby said to its father, 'Why was I born?' or if it said to its mother, 'Why did you make me this way'" (Isaiah 45:9-10, NLT)?

Sweet friend, there is great fulfillment and joy to be found in this life, but it will only come by embracing the unique strengths and gifts He's given you and by using them for His glory. You have something to add to this life that no one else can. Get off the hamster wheel of people pleasing and jump into the rewards of being a God-pleaser by enjoying and using what He has given you.

"Look at the birds. They don't plant or harvest or store food in barns, for your heavenly Father feeds them. And aren't you far more valuable to Him than they are" (Matthew 6:26, NLT)?

"For am I now seeking the approval of man, or of God? Or am I trying to please man? If I were still trying to please man, I would not be a servant of Christ" (Galatians 1:10, ESV).

Closing prayer:

Lord, I want to deepen my understanding of Your great love. Help me to ignore the enemy when he tries to negotiate my value based on his lies. You gave Your life in exchange for mine because You decided I was worth it! Please help me to live in that truth. Thank you! Amen.

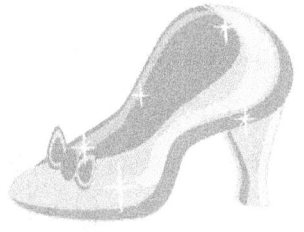

Chapter 3
Performing for Acceptance

"Why should we worry about what others think of us, do we have more confidence in their opinions than in the One who created us?"
~ Brigham Young

It's ironic that I'm writing this chapter while sitting in a place that is so beautiful and peaceful words cannot describe it. I'm overlooking the ocean in all of its splendor. As I soak in the sun and allow the warmth to kiss my skin, I'm overwhelmed with gratitude for this time of relaxation that I'm choosing to experience with pure joy. There's no guilt or shame as I'm breathing in this beauty while simply embracing and enjoying the moment. There's no hustle, personal demands, schedules, or fear that anyone will criticize me for taking time to just relax. I'm thankful for this because rest has become a recent friend bringing refreshing solace to my soul.

Oh, my soul! It has been so horribly mistreated through the years. I can't pinpoint when it all began, but I'll share a glimpse of the world I'm trying hard to escape. Funny how those two words "trying hard" hold the key; they've tripped me up countless times. Like an Achilles heel, it's been a struggle woven through the chapters of my life. So here I am, writing, hoping to untangle the mess so the path ahead is lit with clarity for myself and others to follow. My hope is that redemption will lie in these words and illuminate the way out of any shadows that may be hovering.

Growing up as the middle child of five in a pastor's home, I often felt isolated. My two older sisters were best friends, sharing many interests and activities, but they were several years older than me, so we didn't have much in common. To them, I was just the bratty younger sister. My brother, born three years after me, was the only boy in the family, and although we were closer in age, our interests were completely different. Then there was my baby sister, eight years younger than me, who was too young to hang out with. Despite knowing my parents loved me, I still struggled with loneliness and isolation. The adolescent mind doesn't always arrive at rational conclusions regarding feelings and facts. Adding to my feelings of isolation were the extremely high expectations placed on us as pastor's kids. I'm not bitter; if anything, I'm probably better for it. However, it did create a pattern of striving for perfection in order to gain recognition, a struggle that has followed me through much of my life.

Performance has always been about showcasing the best part of me, exposing only the "good" me to win the praise and love of others. When I would "try hard" to excel in my grades, activities at school or at church, my parents would praise me, and praise is what fueled this drive. Let me interrupt this thought to let you know, I had good parents that sincerely did their very best to not only love us but show us what it meant to authentically live a life of Christian service and dedication to Christ. They are two of the most beautiful, faith-filled Christ followers that I know. They did not create this issue in me; it just added fuel to this issue that I was creating.

It became intoxicating to be praised for something I did, and that can be a dangerous place to live! It's exhausting to always feel compelled to work instead of rest because you're trying to show how valuable you are by outworking, outdoing or outlasting others. I cannot pinpoint the exact moment when I became aware of my problem, but I do know the compulsion to produce and stay busy turned into great frustration in my life.

Just Rest:

My husband took the day off to watch our three young daughters. He was a great dad who loved to get on the floor to play and wrestle, but he wasn't great at keeping things tidy. After a long day at work, I came home to a messy house, toddlers squealing, "Mommy, mommy, mommy," a kitchen with no meal prepared, and a husband who was tired. I immediately jumped into performance mode preparing the meal and settling the kids. Soon after dinner I was drawing baths for our babies and going through the bedtime routines to get the kids in bed.

After getting the little ones to bed, I went into a cleaning frenzy—putting toys away, vacuuming the floor, wiping the table, and heading to the kitchen to tackle the dishes before cleaning up myself. I could hear my husband in the living room, calling for me to come and sit with him, but I ignored his request. Exasperated by my whirlwind of activity, he said, "Babe, can't you come here and just rest?" As much as my body yearned to, my mind wouldn't let me stop. There was just too much to be done to even think about resting. I would rest only when I finally crawled into bed, exhausted, praying none of my children would wake me up through the night. This cycle repeated itself continuously in my life. Even as my children became more independent, there was always something else demanding my time and energy. I felt compelled to accomplish everything on my mental to-do list before I could earn the right to rest. There was more to be done, and never enough time to do it all! In my mind, rest was a non-essential luxury earned only after all tasks were complete!

For so many years I allowed this to push me to invest in the temporal while neglecting the important. The relationship with my husband and children suffered because I was spent doing! Maybe you can or cannot relate. However this hits you, know that God never intended for any of us to live this way. Our lives are not valuable just when we produce; our lives are valuable because Jesus Christ paid an incredibly high price for us. He is the only one who has the right to set our value. Our life, love, and identity need to be found wholly in Christ Jesus, or we will struggle with our worth and the worth of others. I know this, but it is one thing to know something and another thing to live it. I sure wish it wouldn't have taken me so long to start living it. The application of this truth could have saved me so many years of unnecessary struggles. I pray it will spare you of any similar hardships.

> *No matter what stage of life you're in—young, old, married, or single—it's never too late to learn this incredibly empowering lesson: You are loved regardless of what you do! Once you truly understand this, you'll never live another day struggling to prove your worth or fighting for scraps of love from others based on what you "do" for them.*

Beginning my journey toward wholeness:

I was driving home from work one very cold blustering evening while listening to a podcast on the radio. I really needed to stop for gas, but the podcast was so good I didn't want to miss a moment of what was being said so I prayed for the multiplication of gas in my tank. Thank God, I made it home! I do not remember all of what was said, but I do remember the essence of the message was this: when you live from a place of knowing you are completely loved, it frees you from the need to try so hard to earn it. They made the following statement that has stuck with me, "God's love is never based on us, it's simply placed on us."

I had already been in a very real emotional struggle trying to reconcile the truth of God's word with the reality of my life in many areas. This was one of the areas that was so raw and real I knew God was speaking directly to me. I don't think it would have surprised me a bit to hear my name mentioned in the podcast that night. That's how palpable this revelation and truth hit me. I couldn't help but cry, no longer tears of fear, frustration and sadness but rather tears of joy! They washed over me like a refreshing warm shower after a long strenuous workout.

I began to review the beliefs in my own heart regarding God's love. I knew God's love could never be earned or deserved, but there was a disconnect somewhere between the thoughts I believed and the actions I conceived. If this is what I believed, then why was I still trying so hard to earn it? And, from whom? The words of my Grandpa Mac began to ring in my ears: *There's nothing you can do to make God love you any more, and there's nothing you can do to make God love you any less.*

> *Living life in performance mode is like having a relentless taskmaster who gives little rest or reprieve from the constant critique of ourselves and others.*

When you live a certain way for so long, it becomes your normal, and you evaluate everything and everyone through that filter. I'm still growing and surrendering this area of my life. I have to remind myself that I am His workmanship, not my own. He is the Potter; I am the clay. The more I surrender and do not "try" so hard, the more beautiful the outcome. Love is and will always be a greater motivator than fear. When you yield to the transformational love of God it motivates you to love Him back with everything in your life, not out of fear of not being enough but rather gratitude that He is enough!

Lie: I have to earn God's love.
Truth:

"But when the goodness and loving kindness of God our Savior appeared, he saved us, not because of works done by us in righteousness, but according to his own mercy, by the washing of regeneration and renewal of the Holy Spirit, whom he poured out on us richly through Jesus Christ our Savior" (Titus 3:4-6, ESV).

"For by grace you have been saved through faith. And this is not your own doing; it is the gift of God, not a result of works, so that no one may boast" (Ephesians 2:8-9, ESV).

"For it is God who works in you, both to will and to work for his good pleasure" (Philippians 2:13, ESV).

What I love about the previous scripture in Philippians is that, although a life of faith involves works or actions, it doesn't require us to strive for God's approval through our own efforts. Instead, our actions become an overflow of what He pours into us. Learn to rest in His sweet presence; let Him pour into you so that what flows out of you is a rested, revived, and beautiful extension of Him.

Closing prayer:
Thank you, Lord, for providing everything I need to live a free and unshackled life. I am deeply grateful for Your unwavering love that is not based on my actions or abilities. Freely You have given it; now help me to freely receive it and share it with others. Amen.

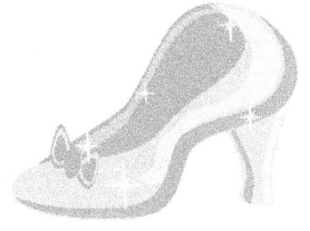

Chapter 4
Not Perfect but Perfecting

"You therefore must be perfect as your Heavenly Father is perfect" (Matthew 5:48, ESV).

Have you ever read a scripture verse that has just stumped you? It left you questioning, what does that mean? Well, the opening scripture was one of those for me. I would reason there's no such thing as "being as perfect as my Heavenly Father". I've tried and failed over and over and a thousand times over again. So why does the word of God ask us to accomplish an impossible task? This scripture literally bothered me. My lack of understanding became another thing feeding my insecurities and quest for the elusive perfection. Instead of perfect, I was left ashamed for not achieving it. I know now that this verse was meant to encourage us to grow and mature, not be flawless.

For years, my struggle with a perfection infection was lurking underneath the surface, eating away at the fibers of the relationships that I loved. The infection that went undetected in me was making the ones around me very sick and the recovery process took a long time to find healing. The revelation of this infection eating away beneath the surface came to light one day while playing an innocent game with friends.

My husband and I have always been big game players. It doesn't matter if it's a board game, a card game, or a team game. We like to play games, and we like to win. On one of our game nights we were playing The Couples Game. This game is set up very similar to the old Newlyweds Game, and I was sure this was going to be an easy win for us. I mean, really, how could we lose? We loved each other, we worked together, and we were raising a family together. This was going to be fun! Separated by a small wall partition, each couple sat facing the host completely blind to their partner. Then came the questions; round 1 had three questions, and I was sure we were leading when the host revealed the results. Question 1 nailed it! Question 2 nailed it! We were on a roll! Now came question 3, "What makes your wife feel incredibly stressed?" My husband answered, cleaning the house. What?!!! I love to clean! Well, maybe not the cleaning part, but I love the results. The crisp clean smell and look when everything is fresh and in its place brings a feeling of peace and order, so I *don't* get stressed! What was making me feel at ease was creating a toxic environment for my family. The constant expectations that everyone needed to participate in my desire for neat, tidy, perfect was creating undue stress on others. My husband shared how my need to have everything in place was making him feel out of place. If he came home and laid his coat on the chair or left his shoes by the door, I would get irritated because my reality was not measuring up to my expectations. My need for perfect was driving a wedge between me and the imperfect family I so deeply loved!

> *My pursuit of a perfect, well-manicured life was keeping me from living well in my actual life.*

I've come to realize there's a significant difference between perfect and perfecting. Perfect represents a cold, plastic image of reality; it embodies the relentless pursuit of fantasy over the warm, inviting and relational aspects of life. In contrast, perfecting means being present in your actual life while recognizing it's worth investing in. Rather than waiting for some fairytale, you fully step in to embrace and thank God for the gift of life, including its messiness. Meanwhile, you maintain an open invitation for the Perfect One to be at the center of your world, providing His strength and grace to make any necessary changes to improve things!

When you're consumed with perfection you will distance yourself from others in fear that they may be exposed to your flaws and see your messy reality; when you are interested in perfecting you will be open to relationships that may see the messiness yet will strengthen, provoke, and encourage you in your journey of growth and development. When we prioritize growth over perfection, we can wholeheartedly contribute to a better world with grace rather than rigid expectations. We'll care less and less about impressing others and care more and more about compassion and love.

> *I've never witnessed a healthy culture of growth and development happen in an environment of criticism and condemnation.*

Let me just say, it's not easy when we have expectations that die hard. We can wrestle our kids, house, marriage, and body into an image of perfection, or we can accept the reality that life is messy, untidy, imperfect, and unpredictable. It is in the beautiful messes that we live, grow and can thrive!

"The Lord will fulfill His purpose for me; your steadfast love, Oh Lord endures forever. Do not forsake the work of your hands" (Psalm 138:8, ESV).

The Apostle Peter is a fascinating case study when it comes to understanding the Lord's great grace and allowance for our imperfections. Jesus spent the last 3 years of His life on Earth with a bunch of hooligans. They were incredibly flawed and broken individuals, men probably none of us would have recruited for our World Changers dream team, yet Jesus did. Not only was Peter volatile but he was also arrogant stating emphatically that he would never deny or abandon Jesus, yet during Jesus most desperate moment on earth, Peter denied Him not once but three times!

If you have ever felt like you have disappointed Christ, betrayed His trust or broken His heart beyond reconciliation, let me assure you, you haven't! Our flaws and failures pale drastically in comparison to His great love and redemption. In John chapter 21 you will find Peter discouraged after his failure. He was ready to go back to his old life, but it's in this place of disappointment that Jesus visits him. Jesus cooks the boys some breakfast and asks Peter a provocative question. In reflection of Peter's denial, He asks. "Peter, do you love Me?" Peter answered, "You know I love You." Three times Jesus asks this question and three times He's met with the same answer. What is brilliantly beautiful in this exchange is the verb tense for love used in this conversation: it differs between Peter and Jesus. The Greek word for love that Jesus uses in this passage is *Agape*. He was literally asking Peter, do you love me perfectly, without flaws and conditions, but Peter responds with the Greek word *Phileo*. "Lord, you know I *phileo* You." *Phileo* love means there's a fondness, affection and friendship love, but it is distinct from *agape* which is sacrificial and selfless.

    Peter had come to the realization that his ability to love could not come close to the perfect, flawless love of God. Jesus asked him again, and with the same response, Peter admits his love is flawed and conditional, not perfect like Christ's love. The third time is the clincher. Jesus was already aware of Peter's limitations and yet asked him again "Peter, do you love me?" but this time instead of *agape*, Jesus used the word *phileo* fully validating Peter's inability to be perfect yet fully accepting him with his limitations and imperfections. Jesus compassionately reassures Peter that He still loves Him and wants to use him.

    Before Peter's denial, Jesus had already called him a rock and prophetically gave him a new identity knowing he would be a great apostle that would carry the gospel of Christ into the known world. By Acts chapter 2, you can see Peter, filled with the Holy Ghost, speaking to thousands about the good news of Jesus Christ. Eventually, Peter even chooses martyrdom over ever denying Christ again.

    Peter was not perfect, but he's a great example of a person perfecting throughout his life. This is my prayer for you, that you would come to the realization that a quest for perfection will forever leave you striving, stressed, and disappointed in yourself for coming up short. Don't throw in the towel or give up on yourself like Peter did before His encounter with Jesus. Accept your limitations; even if your life is messy, it is the only life you'll ever get to enjoy! Don't lose it to a world of unrealistic expectations.

"I am convinced that nothing can ever separate us from God's love. Neither death nor life, neither angels nor demons, neither our fears for today nor our worries about tomorrow—not even the powers of hell can separate us from God's love. No power in the sky above or in the earth below—indeed, nothing in all creation will ever be able to separate us from the love of God that is revealed in Christ Jesus our Lord" (Romans 8:38-39, NLT).

Lie: Perfection is a reality to be achieved.
Truth:

Perfection keeps us working toward an unattainable reality and causes us to wear ourselves out striving for what cannot be achieved. If enjoying your current reality is a struggle, invite the Master Designer into your world and surrender the things you cannot change or control. Allow Him to work in and through the mess to reveal the hidden gems. He may adjust some things in the process to help bring relational, spiritual, or emotional growth, but through His work you will see beauty emerge. Be kind and patient to yourself in the process. You can start today by making the choice to focus on the things that are good in your life and bring you joy. Finally, refuse to carry with you the weight and burden of perfection any longer. Remember, your worth is intrinsic, given to you by God. It is **not** contingent on your achievements or performance. Divine love is rooted in the Creator's actions, not yours.

"Always be full of joy in the Lord. I say it again—rejoice! Let everyone see that you are considerate in all you do. Remember, the Lord is coming soon. Don't worry about anything; instead, pray about everything. Tell God what you need and thank him for all he has done. Then you will experience God's peace, which exceeds anything we can understand. His peace will guard your hearts and minds as you live in Christ Jesus. And now, dear brothers and sisters, **one final thing. Fix your thoughts on what is true, and honorable, and right, and pure, and lovely, and admirable. Think about things that are excellent and worthy of praise**" (Philippians 4:4-8, NLT).

Closing prayer:

Lord, I am far from perfect, and You're okay with that. Thank you for helping me realize that You're more interested in my growth than perfection. Please help me to live authentically, embracing even the messy moments in life so I don't miss the value in any of them. If I am harboring any unrealistic expectations that are stealing joy from my reality, please help me to let them go! Amen.

Chapter 5

Fear Isn't Fair

"Fear is a little dark room where negatives are developed." ~ Michael Pritchard

It was my birthday, and plans were in motion. To my delight, my husband had arranged a day out with no kids in tow. It was just the two of us for the day. First stop was the mall. Forever the gentleman, he pulled me up to the store entrance and said, "Have fun, I'll meet you later." I entered the store, following our familiar routine: he would drop me off at one of my favorite stores, then proceed to one of his own, reuniting at a set time and location to continue our date. Unaware of any deviation in this fun day, I began my shopping adventure. As the designated hour approached, I made my way to the exit, waiting for Mike's arrival, but he didn't appear. I texted him, and his reply assured me he'd be there shortly. When he finally pulled up, I hopped into the car, eager to share my newfound treasures with him.

I immediately sensed something was wrong but could not put my finger on it. I could feel a distance and lack of interest in the air. Later that evening, I used my husband's phone to check on the kids and found images I was completely crushed by. Questions began to swirl like a tornado in my head: why, what, how did this happen? The fear of not being good enough started screaming in my head. We had circled this mountain before, and I thought it was done. Not again, Lord, please not again!

Following this event, fear began to suffocate me, seeping out in undetectable ways. I became hyper-sensitive to his time spent out of my sight; what was he doing? My thoughts would spiral out of control. I concluded that the only way to stop this was to take control. In desperation, I began to micro-manage our world. I set stiff parameters and expected full cooperation. What I thought was good, healthy accountability was becoming a beast in and of itself. I was questioning everything, becoming suspicious of everything, and it was driving a wedge in the relationship I was frantically trying to protect.

What I was doing to manage distance was creating a larger chasm, and fear was driving it all. The fear of losing my husband was growing into a mountain of torment, pushing my thoughts to extremes. I was losing my peace, joy, and grip on the reality of nurturing a healthy relationship with him. Fear thrust the throttle of control into overdrive, and I became overbearing. All the while, fear in my husband was driving him in the opposite direction. The fear and shame he experienced was causing him to retreat into passivity. It was paralyzing him in ways I didn't see until years later. He was so afraid of disappointing and hurting me that he began to hide more of himself, which fed the beast of fear and suspicion in me. Fear was working behind the scenes trying to separate us, desiring to divide and conquer.

In my experience, fear has never fought fair. It fights for complete dominance and control. It has always worked to confine me to spaces and places I was never meant to live. The crazy thing about fear is that it is often undetectable in our own lives because it masquerades itself with different identities. If left undetected, it will keep us from progressing in a healthy direction. We stay stuck, not recognizing that the place it has confined us to is behind a wall of anxiety, shame, low self-esteem, etc. It works to separate us from those who can help us, our heavenly Father, and the people we love.

If you have ever been one to find yourself there, you're not alone. It's been happening since the beginning of humanity.

Let's look at Genesis chapter 3, to help us better understand the way fear works. "And they heard the sound of the Lord God walking in the garden in the cool of the day, and the man and his wife hid themselves from the presence of the Lord God among the trees of the garden. But the Lord God called to the man and said to him, 'Where are you?' And he said, 'I heard the sound of you in the garden, and <u>I was afraid</u> because I was naked; <u>I hid myself</u>'" (Genesis 3:8-10, ESV).

Did you see it? The main reason we hide and withdraw from our heavenly Father and others is fear. Fear of exposure caused Adam and Eve to hide, and fear of exposure is what causes many of us to hide. I have recognized this tendency to withdraw and hide in my own life. I have hidden when I feared people would see my flaws, weaknesses, or failures. We often hide behind a false persona of "everything is good" being careful not to let anyone close enough to see through our masquerade. What we don't consider is the power we give to fear when we allow it to keep us distanced behind a mask.

Fear is such a deceptive tool of the enemy because it disguises itself in real emotions and feelings that can be justified, but I have some good news! When we recognize it, we have the power to overcome it.

"For the weapons of our warfare are not of the flesh but have divine power to destroy strongholds. We destroy arguments (in our minds), and every lofty opinion raised against the knowledge of God, **take every thought captive to obey Christ**" (2 Corinthians 10:4-5, ESV).

God's word is reminding us that we have authority to redirect fearful thoughts and bring down their manipulative power.

> *If we do not take our thoughts, which can produce fearful emotions, captive, they will take us captive.*

Again, fear's goal is to shackle us to a confined space we were never meant to live in. If we do not choose to break out of its shackles, we will surrender our destiny into the hands of our enemy through passivity, manipulation, control, etc.

Friend, if I shared the many times I've allowed the enemy's lying whispers to alter my direction, this would be a very long book. So, let me just sum it up. In the span of my lifetime, I have allowed fear to keep me from pursuing certain relationships, opportunities, schooling, and dreams. Even as I write this book, I have had to push through the bombarding lies that have said, you don't know what you're doing! Why you, why now?! What can you offer that could make a difference? Lies, lies, and more lies, trying to keep me confined to small places, but I am no longer going to let it hold me captive and neither should you. We are pushing through! God's word tells us that satan is a thief, and his only mission is to steal, kill, and destroy (John 10:10). Do not let him destroy your courage, dreams, and destiny.

A few years ago, I read a book called "Lioness Arising" by Lisa Bevere. If you have not read this book, I highly recommend it. Lisa shared a word picture that I have never forgotten. She told the story of some lions that were bred in captivity. When they were old enough to fend for themselves, they removed the boundaries that had once held them captive hoping they would reengage with the wild. The physical barriers were removed, but the mental barriers were still present. Even when they were allowed to explore additional territory, these lions would not journey beyond the line that was once their barrier. They had become so familiar and controlled with their captivity that it took extreme measures by the keepers of the habitat to entice them beyond their invisible confinement. They finally stopped feeding the lions. Instead, they killed a deer and put it downwind, so the hunger would drive them beyond what was once their borders. Isn't that just like us? We get so comfortable being in a place that is familiar it takes extreme measures by our Keeper to entice us to journey beyond our fear-induced boundaries and experience the more He has for us.

We do not have to live in fear and hide our insecurities, sins, and failures from God because He is already fully aware of them and loves us anyway. He loves us right where we are, even if we are currently living in confinement. He loves us too much to let us stay in that place of limitation. If you will just ask and invite Him in, He'll heal you from the lies, ill-spoken words, people-inflicted wounds, and self-inflicted pain. His love is healing and empowering!

"Such love has no fear because <u>perfect love expels all fear</u>. If we are afraid, it is for fear of punishment, and this shows that we have not fully experienced his perfect love" (1 John 4:18, NLT). The more you get to know Jesus and His great love for you, the freer you will become. You've been made for more, but in order to enjoy it you must choose to step into the plush pastures beyond your confinement of fear.

The rest of the story:

It took many years for healing to come to the both of us as wounds had developed from our reactions out of fear. As I sit here today, I can joyfully share that through the struggle, healing has come! I no longer agonize over time separated from my husband. Through exposure and yielding to the healing process, God has helped us form a stronger, better relationship founded on the reality of HIS great love. Though we're not perfect we have a perfect God whose *perfect love expels all fear (1 John 4:17)*. As I close this chapter, I want to expose some fears and lies of the enemy. Recognizing them is a crucial step toward growth and freedom.

The following is a list of some common fears and their disguises:
1. Unknown: Fear of the unknown often convinces us that staying in our comfort zone is safer than venturing

into the unknown. However, growth and transformation occur only when we are willing to step beyond what has been comfortable and familiar.

2. Perfectionism: Fear often masquerades as perfectionism. We fear failure or judgment, so we strive for flawlessness. Remember that imperfections are part of being human. In our journey we will face failure but, *failure is an opportunity to begin again, this time more intelligently ~ Henry Ford.* Don't fear failure; just keep going because progress matters more than perfection.

3. Self-Doubt: This fear whispers doubts about our abilities, worth, and potential. Recognize these thoughts as a disguise of fear and challenge them with the truth of God's word and what He has said about you.

4. Overthinking: Fear thrives on overthinking by playing out worst-case scenarios in our minds. Overthinking can spiral us into a very dark place. If it can get us to believe a worst-case scenario, it will render us stuck and useless because we'll be too afraid to proceed with any action. Practice redirecting your thoughts toward positive outcomes allowing you to move forward.

5. People-pleasing: People-pleasing will make us prioritize other people's opinions over our own well-being be-

cause we fear their critique and judgement. If this is you, learn to set healthy boundaries and don't give other people the power to define you or direct you if it's going to limit you. Disclaimer: God does use people in our lives to help give advice and wisdom, but if their counsel tightens the reigns of confinement or fear they're not the right people to be listening to.

6. Avoidance: This is a type of fear that encourages us to avoid challenges, uncomfortable conversations, or necessary risks. Don't avoid them, rather face them head-on. Often change and growth lie on the other side of our courageous steps of faith.

7. Greed: When we fear loss, we hang on to resources such as time, finances, gifts, and energy to preserve it for ourselves. Unfortunately, in doing so, we lose out on the law of reciprocity. When we sow, we reap later than we sow, more than we sow, greater than we sow. "Give and you will receive. Your gift will return to you in full, pressed down, shaken together to make room for more, running over and poured into your lap. The amount you give will determine the amount you get back" (Luke 6:38, NLT). This is a spiritual law that is irrevocable. Don't let greed limit what God has set up to bless you.

8. Procrastination: This mask of fear will put off doing things, especially hard or unenjoyable things. The root of this action is the fear of failure and fear of missing out. If unchecked, it becomes a thief of your time. It can cause extreme stress, pushing necessary, manageable items into an urgent timeline because it was not taken care of when there was margin. Procrastination pushes things back, assuming there will always be another opportunity, but opportunities are like sunsets; if you wait too long, you'll miss it. "Don't put it off, do it now! Don't rest until you do" (Proverbs 6:4, NLT).

9. Anger: The expression of anger is often a mask over an underlying fear. It can become a default emotion when you fear ridicule, rejection, failure, etc.... If you struggle with anger, become self-aware of your triggers. Ask yourself the why behind the what. Why does that continually trigger anger you? "Whoever is slow to anger is better than the mighty, and he who rules his spirit is greater than he who takes a city" (Proverbs 16:32, ESV).

10. Comparison: The fear of not measuring up drives us to compare ourselves with others. The more we compare ourselves, the more discontented we can become with who we are. Especially in today's Social Media culture of constant exposure, it makes our reality feel insuffi-

cient. Comparison will do one of two things for you; It will either fill you with pride to perceive others as less than, or it will fill you with discontentment when you perceive others are better than you. Either response is not healthy. Paul warned us against this when he said, "We do not dare to classify or compare ourselves with some who commend themselves. When they measure themselves by themselves and compare themselves with themselves, they are not wise" (2 Corinthians 10:12, NIV). We are each too uniquely made by our Creator to compare ourselves to others, so stop!

11. Anxiety: This is an emotional response to fear that causes extreme reactions, much like anger. If not dealt with, it can create ill effects in your mind and body. There are many types of anxieties, but every anxiety is rooted in some form of fear. Be self-aware of the anxieties you may see in yourself and identify the fear it has sprouted from. If you can identify and deal with the core fear, it will annihilate the anxiety. "Humble yourselves, therefore, under the mighty hand of God so that at the proper time he may exalt you, casting *all your anxieties* on Him, because He cares for you" (1 Peter 5:6-7, ESV).

The more truth we are exposed to, the less control and intimidation deception can have. It is important to identify any core fears in your life before you can move past their confinement and experience the freedom that has been purchased for you by Jesus Christ.

"It is for freedom that Christ has set us free. Stand firm, then, and do not let yourselves be burdened again by a yoke of slavery" (Galatians 5:1, NIV).

Jesus came to set the captive free, so don't allow fear to confine or imprison your hope and destiny any longer.

Closing prayer:

Lord, heal my heart and free me from any fear that is holding me back. Help me identify and overcome those fears by shining Your truth into every area of my life. Give me the strength and courage to step boldly beyond any boundaries, fear has created, to receive everything You have prepared for me. Amen.

Chapter 6
No More Hiding

True freedom begins the moment you have nothing to hide.
~ Author unknown

I have been blessed to be the mom of three beautiful girls, both inside and out! I know, moms are notorious for believing their kids are the best (even when they're not). I've been there, but I also recognize that my girls, while beautiful, haven't always behaved beautifully!

When my second daughter was around 3 years old, I felt pretty capable at this "mom thing" and took my two oldest beauties shopping. I went to Walmart for their end-of-season sale where you could buy little girls' dresses, pants, and shirts for less than $3, a deal too good to pass up! During our shopping spree, my youngest, most mischievous toddler, decided it would be fun to spice up our deal hunting with a little game of hide and seek. You probably know where this is going, don't you? She hid in the middle of one of the circular clothing racks unbeknownst to me.

Within a few minutes I realized it was way too quiet to be good, so I turned to check on my girls and Mikayla was nowhere to be found. I felt my heartbeat immediately quicken. Turning to my oldest child, I asked where Mikayla went, but she either didn't know or wasn't telling me (to this day, I'm still not sure). I looked and looked for what seemed to be an hour, but I'm sure it was only a minute. Finally, the terror ended when that little, curly-headed girl began to laugh at my frantic call, and I found her.

The sheer emotion of losing my child had ruined our shopping trip and caused a quick exit from the store. After a stern talk and explanation of why hiding from Mom in a public place is never a good idea, it happened repeatedly in the coming months. Exasperated at trying to get the message through to her, I finally decided to take a different approach.

Being a little wiser, I had learned to keep my eyes on this little girl. The day came again while shopping that she hid in the clothes rack, only this time I saw which one. After calling her name to get her to come out with no response, I hid around a corner. Within minutes, she peeked out to see where mom went, and to her surprise, NO MOM! What had previously been a panicked call from mom to child was now a panicked call from child to mom. The calling out of "mom" got louder and louder until the attention of a sweet clerk came to her aid. With tears flowing down her cheeks, she told the lady she had lost her mom. What she did not know was that her mom was watching the whole thing.

When I finally stepped out from around the corner, this sweet little girl threw her arms around me and asked, "Momma, where were you? I thought you were lost!" What a wonderful feeling it was to be wanted and embraced by this little girl. Her response to me of love and elation melted this momma's heart. The reciprocation of the love I felt for this little girl was great but pales drastically in comparison to what our Heavenly Father must feel when we come running to Him after being lost.

Our lives can look a lot like a big game of hide and seek. I know mine has. Whether it's hiding who we really are from the people around us to fit in or hiding parts of ourselves from our spouse in fear of rejection or maybe we've tried to hide sin, fear, or inadequacy from our Heavenly Father. We stuff our issues beneath a smile so the only thing anyone sees is an image glossed over with a veneer of perfectionism that is rooted in fear.

In preparation for this book, I posed a question to many of my female friends and acquaintances. Actually, I asked a few questions but only one that I will refer to in this chapter. The question was as follows: What is the one thing you fear the most? I was surprised yet not surprised by the common thread that ran through most replies. Over 86% of the responders shared that they feared rejection and abandonment the most. What!? These are beautiful women who are smart and successful, yet they are still struggling with nagging doubts and fears that keep them from living free authentic lives. They hide parts of themselves to avoid rejection and abandonment. We need to consider why this is happening to so many women. Let me share a couple of possibilities I've recognized in my own life.

1. Loss of Identity:

"The thief comes only to steal and kill and destroy. I came that they may have life and have it abundantly" (John 10:10, ESV). Since the beginning of creation, the enemy has worked hard to get us to question who we are and why we're here. Instead of understanding the validity of the Father's love, we look for purpose and identity in other things. When you read the story of how sin entered this world, it wasn't by force but by manipulation. Let's look at what happened in Genesis 3: 1-6. "Now the serpent was craftier than any beast of the field that the LORD God had made. And he said to the woman, 'Did God really say, you must not eat from any tree in the garden?' The woman answered the serpent, 'We may eat the fruit of the trees of the garden, but about the fruit of the tree in the middle of the garden, God has said, 'You must not eat of it or touch it, or you will die.' 'You will not surely die,' the serpent told her. 'For God knows that in the day you eat of it, your eyes will be opened, and you will be like God, knowing good and evil.' When the woman saw that the tree was good for food and pleasing to the eyes, and that it was desirable for obtaining wisdom, she took the fruit and ate it. She also gave some to her husband who was with her, and he ate it" (BSB).

The enemy still works in the same ways today. First, he starts by getting us to question what God has really said or meant by what He said. Second, he will contradict what God has said. Third, he will manipulate the truth, getting us to question the reasoning, opening the door to doubt. Fourth, he'll make the sin look so enticing we'll partake of it forgetting that there are consequences linked to our choices. Just like Adam and Eve, when we fall prey to this deception, it will take us down a road of darkness, shame, and separation from our Heavenly Father.

Notice, that God did not hide from them, but rather they hid from God once they realized the effect of their sin. We are still doing that today. Through sin and shame, we open the door for the thief to come in and accomplish his mission to steal, kill, and destroy. He gets us to question the truth of what the Father has said about us, done for us, and desires for us. If he can make us doubt our Creator, we'll lose our sense of identity and seek for a replacement of His love in all the wrong places.

"I have loved you with an everlasting love; Therefore, with lovingkindness, I have drawn you and continued My faithfulness to you" (Jeremiah 31:3, AMP).

No matter how long you have wondered, come home! No matter how far you have wandered, come home! The Father's arms of love are open for you. Don't continue to struggle with the fear of rejection or abandonment. Stop listening to the lies of the enemy, instead listen and hear the voice of your Father calling you home. It's your place of security and unconditional love — free of fear.

"There is no fear in love, but perfect love casts out fear. For fear has to do with punishment, and whoever fears has not been perfected in love" (1 John 4:18, ESV).

2. Loss of trust:

I'm going to approach this point very carefully and compassionately. Before I share this point, I want to acknowledge that many of you reading this have had very difficult relationships and experiences. I too have had life dish out experiences that I can't easily reconcile emotionally. Some events have left me disappointed and questioning God's goodness. During painful times, it can feel like we've been abandoned and left unprotected, making it hard to trust His Sovereignty. I understand the struggle; I wrote about one of those difficult seasons in chapter 9. But, if we can just hold on, these difficult seasons often lead to some of the most glorious outcomes.

On a lighter note, truth can be challenging to trust. It is one thing to comprehend truth intellectually, but it is completely different to apply truth in application because we trust its outcome. Over the years, I have noticed changes. As I age, certain foods and activities impact me differently than before.

I love summertime in Michigan. With all of its beautiful shorelines you can't help but drive through little beach towns with yummy ice cream shops, and one of my favorite summer treats is a good ole ice cream cone. I do not have one every day or even every week but when I do, I thoroughly enjoy it, until recently. I was on a date with my husband, and we stopped for one of my treats and it did not set right. My body began to react in a way it had never reacted before. I didn't link it to the ice cream; it can't be that! It's my favorite! Surely it must be something else! Fast forward a couple of weeks, and we went out again and ended our date with another ice cream; it happened again but this time worse. Now I was irritated!! "Come on!" I thought to myself. Isn't it bad enough that I've had to give up coffee after a certain hour so I can sleep at night?! I do not want to give this up!! I was arguing with myself, but I was not winning. It finally sunk in when my kids came home for an end of summer get-a-way. We went out for, you guessed it, an ice cream cone; and I had the same reaction!

By this time, I knew the truth and was starting to trust that the response I was experiencing was linked to the ice cream. Applying this knowledge to abstain from ice cream proved to be more challenging. It reminded me of how we often struggle with God's guidance when life serves up unexpected discomforts. We resist change even when we know it's for our good. "For as the body apart from the spirit is dead, so also faith apart from works is dead" (James 2:26 ESV).

> *Truth, no matter how good it is, will only be good for us if we act on it.*

We often know His Word, His heart, and His direction regarding specific things in our lives, but we continue doing what we want because it's familiar, comfortable or simply put, enjoyable. Then when we face the consequences of our choices, we often redirect the blame. I've watched this play out in the lives of so many people, including myself.

Love is more than a noun, and Faith is more than a belief; these are action words that require application. When we humbly surrender in response to God and His ways, it's because we trust Him. When we don't, it's because our trust has been fractured. As we grow in our understanding of God as a loving Father, we realize that His call for obedience is not a killjoy to our fun and freedom but rather a protection from the consequences of poor choices.

I need to preface this next statement by saying, not everything bad that happens in our lives is a result of our poor choices but rather a result of living in a sin-sick, fallen world. The chaos of sin has created a ripple effect that has touched the lives of everyone on this earth. The enemy has convinced many that if God loved them, He would not have allowed (fill in the blank). He wants us to believe that sin's consequence is a lack of the Father's love and care for us. Satan doesn't want us to live with any degree of self-awareness, nor does he want us to see his work of deception and manipulation in the process. Therefore, we tend to blame the very One who loves us most.

Blame shifting can cause us to distance ourselves from our Heavenly Father who has designed and created our lives to have a close relationship with Him. When we lose that connection, it creates a cycle that takes us back to misplaced identity constantly looking for validation in people, places, or things. The stress this creates on those around us, to fill the void, can become overwhelming and will gradually fracture relationships due to the constant pressure. I have been there and done that, but thankfully I have also grown in God's grace. I recognize more quickly when I misplace my identity or trust by anchoring it to things or people. I just run back to my Heavenly Father so He can hold me, heal me, and remind me once again of His perfect love. With Him there is no need to hide.

Lie: Hiding is necessary to protect my heart.
Truth:

"For I am sure that neither death nor life, nor angels nor rulers, nor things present nor things to come, nor powers, nor height nor depth, nor anything else in all creation, will be able to separate us from the love of God in Christ Jesus our Lord" (Romans 8:38-39, ESV).

"The Lord your God is in your midst, a mighty one who will save; He will rejoice over you with gladness; He will quiet you by His love; He will exult over you with loud singing" (Zephaniah 3:17, ESV).

God's word is filled with reminders of His boundless love and never-ending mercies. Let the above verses serve as a compass guiding you home today. Allow this truth to embrace you like a gentle hug protecting you from the lies that keep you hiding. I pray it ignites your soul with new hope as you accept the truth that you can run into the arms of unconditional love without fear. You are and will always be a welcome recipient of the Father's warm embrace.

Closing prayer:
Lord, it's so easy to hide rather than show my flaws. Help

me understand that everyone has imperfections and needs Your grace. Remind me to stay humble, kind, and aware of my dependence on You. When I want to run and hide, pull me back into Your loving arms of peace and protection. Amen.

Chapter 7

I Need Some Grace

"Walk with Me and work with Me, watch how I do it. Learn the unforced rhythms of grace. I won't lay anything heavy or ill-fitting on you. Keep company with Me and you'll learn to live freely and lightly" (Matthew 11:29-30, Message Bible).

When my daughters were young, they absolutely loved dresses, makeup, and pretty shoes. Between the ages of 2 and 8, my house was a constant blur of princess dresses and high heels. They would pull shoes out of my closet to be worn on their tiny feet and prance around the house. They were completely unaware that the shoes they thought were so beautiful were actually quite dangerous because of their ill fit. When I reminisce, it brings a smile to my face as I remember the fun they would have twirling innocently around as if they were Cinderella at the ball. It was cute back then, but now, it would be ridiculous to watch them wear shoes that are too big and act like they are a perfect fit.

As adults, they know their shoe size and what feels comfortably secure on their feet. To settle for something too big or too small would be absurd. What would be even crazier is if they chose to wear those shoes in public. Wouldn't you agree? I can emphatically say, I would never do that! Yet, I have worn a thing or two that has looked ridiculous on me, and I sported it in public!

The girl in the mirror has often looked back at me with bags under her eyes showing the wear and tear of a life that I've tried to neatly manage. Manage?!! Who am I kidding?! Control is more like it! I cannot tell you how often I've tried to wear God's cloak of infinite wisdom, ability, and power. I have tried to control things that only He can control. The dangerous consequences of misfit authority have hurt precious relationships in my life. Instead of living under His grace, I misunderstood and misapplied that grace. Even today I still need God to remind me of WHO is in charge. And then, I remind myself of who does a better job managing everything, me or God? Definitely God! When I step outside of God's sweet grace, all that's left is me.

Frustration was the result I'd manufacture so I would go back to seasons of seeking, praying, and asking the Lord "What would you like to do?" Yet, while I was asking for answers, I was pushing to progress my own agenda. Everything I was striving for seemed good, even God-given, so I'd dive back in pushing, pushing, pushing for it to succeed only to find myself frustrated, exhausted, angry, and ready to quit, again! This has been a repeated rhythm in my life far too many times to even count.

You would think after 50 years of living I'd finally get it, lay down my weakness for His strength and learn to live more within His grace. Instead, I have chosen frenzied and frazzled. Why? That is the question I always come back to, WHY? In the moment, my ways seem much more logical. It's easier, in my humanity, to grab the bull by the horns and try to ride it to my desired destination rather than rest in His grace and timing. Can you relate? God is calling us to live in His *unforced, unhurried rhythms of grace.* If we're going to live in God's grace, we must have a clear understanding of what that grace is. Grace as a noun is defined as the following:

1. Simple elegance or refinement of movement.

2. Courteous goodwill.

3. It is a free, unearned blessing demonstrated in the salvation of sinners.

Grace can also be defined as God's sufficiency and enabling power in the life of the believer. It is His equipping power to do what He has assigned for us to do. God told Paul, "My grace is sufficient for thee: for my strength is made perfect in weakness" (2 Corinthians 12:9, KJV).

Instead of embracing the fact that I have weaknesses, I would cover up my weakness and pretend everything was good. I was working to control the outcome and narrative in my life and the lives of others. I would exhaust myself trying to manage the productivity of my children and even my husband, as if managing my own life wasn't enough. I probably looked a lot like my little girls did when they wore my high heels on their tiny feet, twirling around like my life was perfect, all the while treading dangerously close to a spiritual ankle sprain and strained relationships.

Sometimes, we are conditioned to believe that non-essentials are essential, and we fight to put them on center stage regardless of the cost. I enjoy decorating for the holidays. I like to make things look festive and often have these grandiose ideas that should make the cover of Home and Garden magazine; at least I have great imaginations that they could. What starts as a joy becomes overwhelming in its execution. I used to have great little helpers at home, but they have since grown up and left the homestead, so what's left? Just me and my man. I'd like to think he enjoys decorating as much as I do, but he doesn't. What makes it worse is when he has offered to help, I have often gone behind him and rearranged or removed what I didn't think looked good. It created the impression that his contribution was not necessary therefore leaving me to do this large task alone. Why? I had become an expert at making the non-essential the essential and minimizing what was actually essential — the relationship with my husband. I would get so concerned about the temporary décor of the season that I hurt a precious relationship in the process.

    I have sacrificed more than one relationship on the altar of control in my pursuit of perfection (according to Lynette's standards). I've done it with my husband, kids, and friends. I've been known to give unsolicited advice and go behind others "to fix" what wasn't good enough. When things were out of place, I'd change it under the misunderstood concept of "pursuing excellence," and I'm not just talking about décor anymore.

    When we step outside of God's grace to manufacture our own product, we will be left feeling tired, weary, resentful, and ready to quit. I was there! That's when God, in His great mercy, began to show me the times I ran ahead without His grace equipping me for the task of working with the people I love. His grace is what helps me make allowances for other people's personalities, gifts, contributions, and even weaknesses, like He does for mine. It's humbling to admit, yet so freeing to realize that He loves me no matter how crazy I have looked wearing His shoes of control.

I'm still a work in progress learning to lay back and not go all gangbusters with my own agenda and expectations. I've been a hard nut to crack! I wish I wouldn't have hurt precious people while running ahead of God's grace, but I'm grateful that today is a new day of mercy and grace for each of us.

"Because of the LORD's great love we are not consumed, for his compassions never fail. They are new every morning; great is your faithfulness" (Lamentations 3:22-23, NIV).

In preparation for one of our annual women's conferences, I was praying for a theme and direction for ministry. The Lord gave me the following that I believe fits so well here. "Dear sister, have you ever heard the phrase 'you are enough'? It sounds so encouraging, but if we're not careful it can pull us into a life of self-sufficiency that keeps us striving, isolated, and weary. Your Heavenly Father wants to set you free from the lie that you have to be enough. Jesus is the only ONE who is enough. Our strength is limited, but He is unlimited! He wants you to know that it's okay to not be enough because He is enough for you!"

Lie: I can do it all on my own.
Truth:

"But if it is by grace, it is no longer on the basis of works; otherwise, grace would no longer be grace" (Romans 11:6, ESV).

"And God is able to make all grace abound to you, so that having all sufficiency in all things at all times, you may abound in every good work" (2 Corinthians 9:8, ESV).

This verse in 2 Corinthians used to be a bit of a mystery to me. By simply reading it, it sounds as if I should be able to successfully manage and do all things, at all times, without weariness, frustration, or limitation, but that is not the context. In studying this verse, I have come to realize it's referring to every good work He's specifically assigned for us to do with His grace. We're not assigned to everything and everyone; so, in keeping with God's rhythms of grace, know your assignment.

> *Your assignment will often be your God-given bend. What are you gifted for? What is your pure, genuine life passion? Those passions, people, and projects are what encompass your assignment. It is your life's "what, who, and why."*

If you are struggling to pinpoint your assignment, ask the Creator. "If you need wisdom (insight, knowledge, direction), ask our generous God, and he will give it to you. He will not rebuke you for asking" (James 1:5, NLT).

The Creator of this universe has created each of us to thrive in this life. He doesn't want you to walk under the weight of unrealistic expectations, mismanaged control, or misaligned assignments that will lead to frustration. Rather, He wants you to live in the specific grace He's given you to fully live, love, and make a glorious impact in this world that He's made for you!

Closing prayer:

God, You know my weaknesses but still chose me. Thank You for that! When I see faults in others, help me to respond with love and compassion instead of criticism or shame. Direct my focus toward what is right rather than what is wrong, so my hope stays intact. Thank You for Your grace and for helping me to extend that grace to others. Amen.

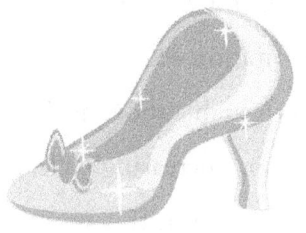

Chapter 8

Invited But Not Really

"Rejection steals the best of who I am by reinforcing the worst of what's been said to me." ~ Lysa Terkeurst

"Yeah, somehow, we forgot to invite you. I'm sure you could still get a room if you'd like to come, but our room is full." I hung up after this conversation, wondering why she even bothered to call and tell me about this weekend trip coming up one week before the event. I was the odd one out, a secondhand thought for a girl's getaway that used to be open to my participation. It was the second year in a row that I was invited on a whim. Maybe the invitation was delayed in hopes that I wouldn't be able to attend with such a short notice. I was invited but *not really*. It was becoming increasingly clear to me that I was no longer a welcome addition in this group of friend's activities, and the realization hit with a sting. Not understanding in full, I wondered, "Lord, what's going on?!" That question gnawed at me. My journey with God has often been filled with questions, but not instantaneous answers. Much of the time, the answer is revealed through a process, which is what happened here, but I'll return to the process in a moment.

This is a good place for me to give you some encouragement. If you're like me and can relate to this scenario, it can flood your being with the emotions of what remembering rejection can bring. I used to dread the old playground games that were played in teams. I wanted to play and be included with the others, but I was often the last one picked. Even as a child, I remember the sting of rejection when no one wanted me on their team. Looking back, I understand a little better now. I was gangly, awkward in my development, and not very athletic. As hard as I tried to be a valuable player, it just wasn't reciprocated with a ready invitation.

Rejection can haunt you with insecurity and fear even in your adult life, but let me remind you, there is absolutely NO

ONE who defines your value, importance, and purpose more than your Heavenly Father. He has not only invited you into His family but has lavished His great love on you, yes YOU! He is so interested in all the details of your life and existence that He has even numbered the hairs upon your head, even the ones that fell out and gathered in your shower drain this morning.

"What is the price of two sparrows, one copper coin? But not a single sparrow can fall to the ground without your Father knowing it. And the very hairs on your head are all numbered. So, don't be afraid; you are more valuable to God than a whole flock of sparrows" (Matthew 10:29-31, NLT). Good news, right? You're not just more valuable; you're more beautiful also.

  I have lived much of my life striving! Striving for love, validation, and acceptance, looking for a place my heart could call home. I longed for a place where I could be fully known and still fully loved with all my imperfections. It's funny to even write "fully known" because the truth is, I have struggled with my ability to be vulnerable and open to any person except my Heavenly Father. Thankfully, He's been so gracious and loved me through my insecurities even when I didn't recognize it.

  I wanted to obtain the caliber of God's love and acceptance from others but would come up empty. I was seeking to fill the enormous hole in my soul with family and friends, continually disappointed by their inability to do so. I didn't recognize that, just like me, they are human, flawed, broken in places, wounded, scarred, and looking for their own place of refuge. Humanity, at its best, is still desperately needy. We are incomplete and incapable of giving unconditional love and acceptance to each other. Do not misunderstand what I'm trying to say. We can give love and acceptance but outside of the enabling grace of Jesus Christ, there will always be conditions.

It has taken me a lifetime of work and struggle, but I have finally realized that the rejection I have felt throughout my life is what has pushed me into a deeper relationship with my Heavenly Father. This beautiful relationship is a place I may not have voluntarily gone to if my security had been found in anyone or anything else.

The Process:

Now, let's go back to the process I referred to earlier. Whenever God begins to shift things in our lives it can get uncomfortable; this is where I was at. Uncertain of what God was doing through this pulling away of friends, I began to withdraw from other friendships outside of my family. Not that I wasn't friendly or concerned about others, but I was guarded in an effort to protect my heart from the hurt of rejection and disappointment again. It stayed that way until a casual conversation with a friend. She randomly mentioned, "There are some relationships in life that are only meant to be close for a season. God will bring separation in some relationships to make room for others. This will shift us in ways that will bring about a different outcome in our life." It was as if the Holy Spirit just called an audible, and I was finally listening. I was guilty of trying to nestle into what was a familiar, cozy, comfortable place in life, but God wasn't going to let me stay there. He had other plans, better plans than what I was settling for, so He was allowing things to get uncomfortable to get me to move, grow, and lean into Him more.

"In a desert land, he found him, in a barren and howling waste. He shielded him and cared for him; he guarded him as the apple of his eye, like an eagle that stirs up its nest and hovers over its young, that spreads its wings to catch them and carries them aloft" (Deuteronomy 32:10-11, NIV).

In the animal kingdom, an eagle's parenting skills may seem extreme! When a baby eaglet gets big enough to fly, catch their own food, and become self-sufficient, the momma will begin to rustle up the nest and make their cozy, comfy existence uncomfortable until the eaglet finally decides to fly. But make no mistake; momma isn't far behind. She stays at a close enough distance to assist just in case the eaglet begins to plummet. She will then swoop in, rescue the eaglet, and bring him back to safety. This process may repeat itself several times but eventually, the eaglet gets confident and capable enough to finally soar. This is what God was doing in my life. He was rustling up the nest I had grown comfortable with in order to get me to fly.

What is your Heavenly Father allowing to get uncomfortable in your life right now because He's wanting you to soar rather than stay in a comfortable nest depending on others to feed your hunger? I pose this question with the hope that you will open your heart to the possibilities that lie before you if you dare to trust His nudge. His gentle push is to get you to move where you have resisted going. You are not alone; we all have spaces and places in our lives that need growth and development. Let the uncomfortable places draw you closer to the only one who can nurture your growth and lead you to something beautiful on the other side of the pain.

The woman at the well: *John 4:4-30 (Church history refers to her as Fatima.)*

It was another trip under the relentless, midday sun, as Fatima trudged to the well, she felt the weightiness of the water jugs she was carrying on her shoulders. Each step was a reminder of her daily torment. Of course, this trip would be much more comfortable in the cool of the morning or evening hours, but the townspeople were active at those hours and their disdain for her was etched into her soul. Because of her unholy reputation, she was never welcome to walk with the other women in the village.

She had grown all too familiar with the heat. When she finally reached the well, sweat was cascading off her brow and her throat was parched. Oblivious to the world around her she was ready to scoop up some cool water to quench her thirst when a voice pierced her solitude. Startled by his voice she stopped. "Is he speaking to me?" she wondered. Stealing a quick glance, she was surprised she was not alone. No one ever ventured here at this hour, yet a Jewish man was addressing her.

It was his gentle voice that caused her to lift her gaze and listen to his request. Many men had requested much from her, but he was different. All he wanted was water. Both annoyed and relieved at his request, she began to converse with this stranger. She couldn't remember the last time a man spoke to her with such kindness, "He doesn't know me!" Oh, but he did! This man didn't just know her reputation, he knew her. He saw beyond her reputation, beyond the whispered judgments. He saw her.

Then, astonishingly, he began to reveal her past, present, and future. Instead of ridicule and shame, Fatima felt an overwhelming love from this stranger. "Could this be the Messiah?" Indeed, the Messiah had come to meet with her—a voiceless Samaritan—to introduce him to her town. With his words, he healed more than her thirst; he healed her soul and invited her into his plan of redemption and grace.

This transformative encounter not only altered Fatima's life but touched the lives of many in and beyond her town. It happened in a place of desolation for a woman who was rejected and unwelcome in the normal activities of others. In that place of isolation, the Savior met her, healed her, and commissioned her.

> *Being uninvited in the "normal" activities of others can feel lonely, but it may be the very place where God is waiting to meet with you.*

He is prodding you so that He can send you into new territory. Don't be afraid; He'll never abandon you on this journey. He'll meet you right where you're at. If you're feeling rejected and uninvited, He is inviting you into His perfect love and plan for your life. If accepted, His invitation will lead you to something far greater than the comfortable place you want to reside. Being comfortable may be easier, but it's NOT better! Just like the eagle, He's wanting to push you out of your nest of comfortable excuses and get you to fly.

As God worked through Fatima, He desires to work through each of us. Consider the following ways an encounter with Jesus can change you:

1. Weakness is replaced with strength: Remember the words of Philippians 4:13: "I can do all things through Christ who strengthens me" (NKJV). When you feel inadequate or overwhelmed, God's strength empowers you to face every challenge. He sends the voiceless with his voice, the rejected with his approval, and the broken with His healing. Your weaknesses become the opportunities needed for His grace to shine.

2. Purpose emerges: "For it is God who works in you to will and to act in order to fulfill his good purpose" (Philippians 2:13, NIV). God has a plan and will even work through adversity to shape your desires and actions to facilitate His good purpose within you. Trust His guidance and let Him lead you toward something even more beautiful and purposeful.

3. There's impact on others: Just as Fatima's encounter at the well impacted her community, your life can and will influence those around you. God speaks through His children, using their words and actions to touch hearts and change lives. Be open to being a vessel for His message allowing your life to become HIS story for others to read. Let God work through you, transforming your struggles into strengths and disappointments into new directions, guiding your steps to impact those around you in beautiful ways.

Lie: Uninvited = rejected
Truth:

Uninvited in one place does not mean you're uninvited at His place. In opposition to rejection, His presence becomes a richer, more inviting place for the soul to find solace and a beautiful place to call home.

"You make known to me the path of life; in your presence, there is fullness of joy; at your right hand are pleasures forevermore" (Psalm 16:11, ESV).

"The Lord is near to the brokenhearted and saves the crushed in spirit" (Psalm 34:18, ESV).

"For the Lord will not forsake his people; he will not abandon his heritage" (Psalm 94:14, ESV).

"The Spirit and the Bride say, 'Come.' And let the one who hears say, 'Come.' And let the one who is thirsty come; let the one who desires take the water of life without price" (Revelation 22:17, ESV).

Closing prayer:

Father, the pain of rejection is real and sometimes it's hard for me to let it go, but today I am making a choice to release the hurt, bitterness and any unforgiveness so my heart can heal. Bring Your peace where there's been chaos and healing where there's been pain. Rebuild trust in my heart and help me to embrace what You have planned for my life. Amen.

Chapter 9
Better Broken

"When you go through deep waters, I will be with you. When you go through rivers of difficulty, you will not drown. When you walk through the fire of oppression, you will not be burned up; the flames will not consume you" (Isaiah 43:2, NLT).

I was finally home after a busy day at work. My body was tired, and I was looking forward to relaxing after an exhausting day of ministry when my phone rang. Scrambling to find where I had laid it down, I saw a number I did not recognize. "Should I answer it?" The thought of ignoring it crossed my mind, but I quickly dismissed the thought and answered. I heard someone ask. "Is this Lynette?" "Yes", I replied, and within seconds, I recognized the voice on the other end was a longtime friend of my parents; I could hear the concern in her voice. "Lynette, your parents have been in an accident." What?!! My mind began to whirl. I had just spoken with my parents earlier that day.

Finally, I asked, "Are they okay?" Unfortunately, the caller had very little details on the current condition of my parents. She had only received secondhand information from her husband who had been at the scene of the accident. She reassured me she would call me back if there was anything more she could find out. "Okay", I said, and we hung up after a brief exchange of necessary information.

They say a father is a girl's first superhero, and for me, that was surely true. My dad was a rock! He was a true patriarch and leader in our family. He had been a faithful protector, father, husband, and pastor. He was the one we would always run to for advice, prayer, wise counsel, and any other concern that left us wondering. From the age of 13 my dad had felt the call of God on his life to love and lead people. He had served faithfully for 28 years as a pastor in a small community because of his love for God and the people. Now, we were pastoring the same church he had planted 51 years prior.

Family roots run deep in this small community church where he raised all 5 of his children to serve with the gifts and talents God had given us. Strength and stability were built as a result of his longevity there. He had developed a reputation of being a father to many. Anyone in need of encouragement or advice could seek an audience with him. He was filled with compassion and kindness tangible to everyone around him. Why am I telling you this? Because this story needs a foundation for you to understand the magnitude of what is to come.

    I was wrestling with best and worst-case scenarios, but the best-case scenario won out. I had not called my siblings yet as I was still waiting for details and did not want to concern them with any unnecessary worry. Finally, after an hour had passed, I called back only to be told they were both taken to the hospital, but they didn't know where.

    I immediately Googled the phone numbers of hospitals in Tulsa, Oklahoma looking for any information I could find. I reached the emergency room of a big city hospital that recognized the name of my parents and put me on hold. Great! Now I'll know what's going on. Soon, a nurse from the emergency room picked up the line to inform me in detail of what had happened to my parents. They were not *in* a car accident as I had expected, but they were in an accident. My parents were crossing a busy intersection when a truck pulled out of a store parking lot. Not seeing my parents, he zoomed out into the lane and hit both of them. The mirror on the truck clipped my dad's head while the fury of the impact hit my mom's scooter throwing her 40 feet from impact. The nurse proceeded to explain that my parents were both conscious and looking fairly good for what they had been through. They were going to continue to evaluate them and would call me back if there were any concerns or emergencies that developed through the night. I hung up feeling relieved and decided it was time to call my siblings to explain the situation and get them to pray for their recovery.

Thursday morning arrived, and since I had not been informed of any concerns throughout the night, I left for work. You ever have this nagging feeling that something isn't right? Well, I did but ignored it realizing the hospital had my number, so surely, they would have called if there were any concerns! Around 10 am I just couldn't ignore the feelings any longer. From work, I called the hospital and was immediately told to hold as the doctor needed to speak with me. Within minutes, the doctor was on the phone explaining that throughout the night, the swelling in my dad's brain had increased, and they could not get him to respond to anything. "Mrs. Beeler, this is serious, and I need to know if it would be okay to do surgery and remove part of your father's brain to alleviate the pressure?" "What?! When did this happen? Why didn't anyone call me earlier?" The questions were flowing. I explained that I have siblings I must consult because I do not want to make this decision alone. After a quick conference call with my siblings, we decided to trust the Lord for dad's healing.

Thirteen years prior, my dad faced the same choice regarding my mom who had suffered a severe stroke. At that time, he said, "If the Lord is going to heal her, it will be with all of her brain." After informing the doctor of our decision, he suggested that we make plans to come and see him. We did, and after a 12-day battle for survival, my dad passed away, leaving a huge hole in the hearts of all who knew and loved him.

> *Tragedy and loss will strike all of us at some point in life, but how we face it will either build us or break us.*

We can hold on to this world so tightly; it's devastating when things shift, and life becomes different or difficult. Many of us have believed that, as Christians, we should be exempt from heartache and pain. Then, when pain strikes, it shakes us at the core of our faith. We forget that the most righteous and perfect of humanity died a very gruesome, lonely death, but it was not in vain! His pain became our gain. What I know about God is He never wastes pain as deep and wide as it spans, He is the Master Redeemer who repurposes pain to surface new purpose.

"That is why we never give up. Though our bodies are dying, our spirits are being renewed every day. For our present troubles are small and won't last very long. Yet they produce for us a glory that vastly outweighs them and will last forever! So, we don't look at the troubles we can see now; rather, we fix our gaze on things that cannot be seen. For the things we see now will soon be gone, but the things we cannot see will last forever" (2 Corinthians 4:16-18, NLT).

After spending 10 days at the hospital, watching my dad cling to life by a thread, witnessing my mom's pain and disability prevent her from fully processing it all, observing my siblings' emotions swing from anger to sadness to compassion for my mom and others, to planning the memorial service, I was spent! On top of everything, we now had the full responsibility of caring for my mom because the stroke had left her severely disabled on her left side. My dad was not only her companion but full-time caregiver, and now he was gone. My world was being turned upside down! During a season I was supposed to be celebrating the high school graduation of my youngest child, her new college career, and the soon-to-be enjoyment of empty nesting, my life was being thrown into a chaos I didn't expect nor ask for.

I could feel myself suffocating under the magnitude of it all. This is not what I thought my life would look like in this season. I had been planning to step into a new season of freedom where my schedule was going to shift, leaving more time for the things I enjoyed but had placed on the back burner for a very long time. Now, I could see it slipping through my fingers. I didn't know how to articulate my feelings to my husband or my family. All I knew, for sure, was my life was changing in ways I had not planned and could not control. My reality was choking out my long-awaited expectations.

My husband was going through his own grief. He was feeling the weightiness of baby number 3 leaving home and moving 3 states away. His spiritual mentor and friend was gone, and now his normally cheerful wife was feeling overwhelmed with her new responsibilities, leaving little time or attention to direct his way. With concern for me and us, he decided a day away is just what we needed.

He planned a sweet Saturday morning escape to a place he knew I'd enjoy. Soon after arriving, I felt my breath getting shallow, my chest tightening, and my head spinning. What was going on?! Our date ended abruptly when my husband took me to the hospital. After a thorough examination, I found out I was completely fine! The stress of everything had brought me to a breaking point in the form of a panic attack!

This could not be happening! What about my dreams, my plans? Surely God had given me those desires, so why this upset?! Why did my dad have to die during an already life-changing season? Why did my mom have a stroke that left her needing full-time care? Why were my children all moving out of state? Why was my mind playing tricks on me causing my body to respond in disabling ways? WHY?? There were so many questions and I wanted answers to ease the pain. I was mad, mad at God for allowing things to happen without considering the consequences on me and my family. Yes, I thought that, but hold on because my circumstances, questions, and anger were taking me to the very place I needed to be … Broken!

Broken:

> *Like a mosaic it's the broken pieces that are gathered to form a masterpiece.*

We often think being broken is a terrible thing when, in reality, it can be the best thing we could ever experience. Without being broken we won't seek the Healer and Restorer. I do not understand my humanity on this. I love God and seek to serve Him, but there's nothing like a good crisis to break down my self-sufficiency and pride. Nothing exposes my not-enoughness more than brokenness. When I finally get to the end of myself, I reach up and grab ahold of the only source of real hope and help, Jesus!

God doesn't need me to be strong. He doesn't need you to be strong either. We often have the misconception that for God to love us and use us, we need to get ourselves together. We have believed that if we're weak, we're unusable or unnecessary, but this belief is a lie! It does not line up with scriptural truth, yet many have believed this lie and therefore disqualified themselves from the very purpose for which they were created.

God's word clearly states, "But God chose what is foolish in the world to shame the wise; God chose what is weak in the world to shame the strong" (1 Corinthians 1:27, ESV). Why!!? Why would God dare to use foolish, weak things to accomplish His work? Because broken, weak things realize they are incapable of doing anything great outside of the God-factor. It causes us to live in humility and dependency on the true source of our strength. Even the Apostle Paul addressed this. In 2 Corinthians 12:7-9, you see him recognizing his weakness to boast and be arrogant. Therefore, God allowed a thorn in the flesh to keep him from boasting in himself but rather in the sufficiency of God.

Moses is another biblical example of humility through adversity. We know, by scripture, that Moses must have been a good-looking individual (Exodus 2:2). He was adopted into royalty with every possible luxury and provision; he didn't need to work or struggle for anything. I believe that is part of the reason God allowed Moses to be afflicted with a speech impediment. It would have been very easy for Moses to be arrogant, but God had other plans which required a humble servant. God's assignment was to raise him up as a deliverer and pastor for His people.

When God finally revealed his plan to Moses, Moses couldn't see how God could use him! He had every excuse in the book for God to look elsewhere. Moses couldn't get past his impediment (his weakness). He wrestled with inadequacy, yet that is exactly what God allowed for his humility so Moses wouldn't think HE could do anything but rather would surrender to the Great I Am to do it through him. We know the rest of that story, Moses, indeed became a great leader because he understood his strength and wisdom came from the Lord alone. He had a holy dependency on God for the duration of his lifetime. When you read Exodus 33:12-23, you see Moses still relying on God, petitioning for His presence, and even making a pretty bold request in verse 15, "If Your presence does not go with us, do not lead us up from here." His desperate need for God and His presence gained him access to a relationship with the Lord that very few people ever experience. He was able to speak face to face with God as a friend (Exodus 33:11).

> *God knows that our humanity is selfish and fiercely independent wanting to prove ourselves and show that our strength and sufficiency is enough. We put on this façade of strength and perfection, afraid to let anyone in on our secret sins, fears, or failures, but the overwhelming awareness of our own weakness comes to light in struggle and crisis.*

This is where I was at...

A few weeks after my breakdown, I was at a pastor's conference in Texas. On the first night of the conference, there was a worship service allowing church leaders to just sit, soak, and refresh in the presence of the Lord. I was sitting there, still numb, confused, and angry. Even though I was surrounded by thousands of pastors, in an environment of great faith, I felt my faith was small. I was still struggling to come to terms with my dad's death. I had no answers as to why God didn't heal him. I sat depleted, questioning whether I should even be in ministry! If I couldn't pray and see a miracle for my dad, how could I pray and expect a miracle for anyone else? As if a miracle depends on me?!

Surely, after years of ministry experience, I should have seen God preparing something through all of this, but I didn't; I was blind-sided. I sat in the crowd as the song *Way Maker* began to play. A song I had loved now came as a slap in the face. Way Maker? Really? Why didn't you make a way in my dad's hospital room? A thousand arguments began to circulate through my head. I was standing face to face with my doubts, fears, anger, and questions of God's sovereignty, goodness, and power. It was as if a spotlight of epic spiritual proportion was shining down on all of my thoughts, and I broke. Unable to answer the questions that had taken me down a long dark road of doubt, I could no longer hold it together. I broke! And it wasn't a nice, clean, tidy break but a shatter. I exploded with emotions so deep and intense all I could do was sob, an ugly, snotty, loud sob. It was so intense I couldn't even stand, and the more I tried to control it, the uglier it got.

God began to reveal the brokenness of my sin: my self-righteousness that made me feel entitled to answers that only eternity is privy to. My thinking had become a toxic dump of doubt, and God was stepping in. Through all the noise, He got my attention. What I heard, took me by surprise. I heard Him say, "Lynette, you can trust Me." "What?!" I started to argue, my thoughts were screaming. "No, I can't! You hurt me, abandoned me, left me in this mess." But the more I tried to argue, the louder I heard Him whisper into my spirit, "You can trust Me." For every doubt and question, I raised, it was met with this same response, "You can trust Me." I don't even know how long I wept or how loud I had become; the only thing I remember is the service ending and complete strangers coming over to pray for me as they exited. Normally, this would have been humiliating, but in this moment, it was the Lord completing His washing over me, extracting every lie, toxic thought, and emotion that had held me captive. I was getting free and free felt wonderful! I felt anger melt off, fear melt away and the sweetest peace wash over my soul. He was breaking me, but this broken was beautiful!

Lie: God needs me to be strong.
Truth:

1. Our God invites all of us to a place of tender intimacy and holy dependency on Him, but we have a choice. We can either wrestle with the Creator of the universe for control or we

can surrender. In my experience, surrender is sweeter and brings much more peace.

2. Adversity will come, but our God has promised He would be with us through it all. Our only responsibility is to lean into Him, trust Him, and obey Him. There's something beautiful on the other side of adversity so hold on!

"He will provide for those who grieve in Zion – to bestow on them a crown of beauty instead of ashes, the oil of joy instead of mourning, and a garment of praise instead of a spirit of despair. They will be called oaks of righteousness, a planting of the Lord for the display of His splendor" (Isaiah 61:3, NIV).

"He has made everything beautiful and appropriate in its time. He has also planted eternity [a sense of divine purpose] in the human heart [a mysterious longing which nothing under the sun can satisfy, except God] – yet man cannot find out (comprehend, grasp) what God has done (His overall plan) from the beginning to the end" (Ecclesiastes 3:11, Amplified Bible).

If you're sitting in a season of brokenness, please know you are NOT alone; the Savior is right there with you, and He will not abandon you. Let His sweet Truth wash over your soul as He whispers, "Fear not, for **I am with you**; be not dismayed, for I am your God; I will strengthen you, I will help you, I will uphold you with my righteous right hand" (Isaiah 41:10, ESV).

Closing prayer:

Jesus, it's difficult to see beauty after experiencing pain. My heart has been broken, but I believe You are the One who can mend what's been damaged. Please help me to grieve in a way that leads to healing. I pray You will bring the right people into my life—those who will support me when I feel weak and shine Your light when everything seems dark. I believe You still have wonderful things planned for me; please help me to hold onto that hope. Amen.

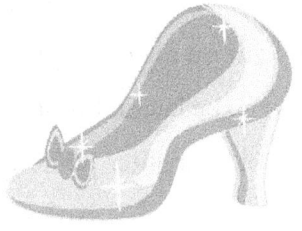

Chapter 10
A Little Margin Goes A Long Way

"The best things of life are written in the margins." ~ Author Unknown

"Devoting a little of yourself to everything means committing a great deal of yourself to nothing." ~ Andy Stanley

It was no ordinary Sunday morning as I slipped into my office for a few moments of quiet before the service was to start. The morning was especially rare because I was not scheduled for any ministry responsibilities that my normal Sunday would consist of. As I sat there in meditation and prayer, I happened to notice the blinking light on my office phone, which alerted me to a voicemail waiting to be heard. I pushed the button to listen and heard my 8-year-old daughter politely ask if I knew where her black dress shoes were; she was getting ready for church and couldn't find them.

Normally, this would have frustrated me. Why? Because much of my life was a whirlwind of responsibilities, expectations, and activity that often left me frazzled. When my reality did not measure up to my expectations, it left me frustrated. My daughter, not knowing where her shoes were on a usually busy Sunday morning would have thrown this mom into a frustrated tizzy because it was one more thing I would have to do. My already loaded plate would have spilled over as anger onto this sweet child.

Thank God it did not, not that day anyway! As I heard her apologetic voice asking, ever so sweetly, if I had seen them, hot tears poured down my cheeks, not because of lost shoes, but because of the encounter I had with myself. The vision in my mind saw me reacting out of my normal frustration, and I was ugly! No wonder that sweet voice sounded so apologetic, she had encountered my hostility before and didn't want to poke the bear.

As I sat there crying, I repented not only to my Heavenly Father for the poor example I was setting for my girls, but I also repented to myself for spending so much of my time and energy running here and there ... doing, doing, doing ... thus, making me exhausted, irritable and anxious! It was at this moment that I prayed for change. This was not who I wanted to be, nor what I wanted my kids to remember me for. As I sat at my desk, the prayer of repentance came so freely and so did the tears. I'm sure when I walked into the sanctuary that morning my eyes were red and puffy, but I honestly didn't care because I was done with me as me; I was ready for change!

Ready? Yes, but how and where do I start? The argument began ... Wasn't this the norm? The quintessential life of a young mother—busy, deeply involved, always on the move, perpetually exhausted. Did I mention busy? Weren't all moms, just like me, stretched to their limits, with little time and energy to spare? When life demands every waking moment, you just can't stop! There are things to do: a house to clean, a family to manage, schedules to navigate, a church to serve, and a job to work at. This busy pace was necessary to keep up with the ever-growing to-do lists and over-crowded schedules which left a really small margin for rest, replenishment, and refueling. This was my life. I justified my frenetic existence based on unrealistic expectations I'd internalized as truth. But it wasn't truth; this lie of striving to do it all while acting like it was no big deal was stretching me to the brink of disaster, making me irritable with those closest to me. "This has to stop!" I cried. "Lord, please help me!"

The Lord was answering my prayers when a few weeks later I pulled into the garage with a car filled with groceries. My weekly shopping trip created more bags than I could carry alone. My girls were with me so in an effort to be helpful they each grabbed a bag or two. My youngest child decided she would grab the gallon of milk, which was too heavy for her to handle, but she grabbed it anyway. On her way into the house, she dropped the milk, which exploded everywhere! There was milk on the steps, the welcome mat, the floor underneath, and her. My initial thought when I saw the mess was to scold her sternly for trying to carry something too heavy to handle, but the Holy Spirit stopped me in my tracks. I heard Him whisper, "Don't scold her, embrace her." She already felt bad and by this time was crying for dropping the milk. I very gently responded to the Holy Spirit and knelt by my child to hug her. I instantly saw the surprise on her face as she sweetly looked up and responded, "Mommy, I'm sorry. I thought I could carry it." "It's okay, honey. I know it was an accident, now let's clean it up." This interaction was so sweet, I couldn't believe how the Lord helped me respond soft rather than harsh and frustrated. Now, if only this person could stay.

This is why margin is necessary to build into our lives.

> *We cannot maintain a frantic pace without it affecting our peace, well-being, and the relationships around us.*

When we are at peace, we have a greater capacity to respond appropriately to unexpected diversions, distractions, and disasters rather than with an instinctive reaction.

So, what exactly is margin? Margin is a delicate balance between responsibilities and the boundaries that hold things together and create more freedom. It's the space needed to avoid breaking points, a momentary pause where we can catch our breath. Imagine it as the tranquil gap between a deep inhale and a satisfying exhale, a place where exhaustion retreats and vitality is revived. The need for margin is woven into the very fabric of our existence. In essence, margin is the antidote to overload giving us balance and peace.

Embracing margin means reserving precious moments in the day for rest. This isn't just physical but also mental rest. It's a recuperation period needed for our minds and emotions.

> *Quality rest is a lifeline for your well-being emotionally, physically, and spiritually.*

When fatigue walks in, faith walks out. ~ Dr. Lester Sumerall. Overcommitted schedules and fatigue can make you irritable with others, and coffee just isn't enough to mend the weariness; only rest can.

Even after the excuse of raising children passed, I still struggled with the intentional practice of rest. The Lord continued to patiently remind me that until I listened and obeyed His directive, I would continue to struggle with fatigue physically, emotionally, and spiritually. The constant need to do was taking its toll and I had to make some choices to shift my attitude on prioritizing rest.

I'm not an expert, rather a work in progress, but let me share some practical ways I've learned to incorporate a little more margin in my own life:

1. Plan more time in your schedule for tasks. I remember, as a young mom, I would often underestimate the time it takes to get everyone ready, this would leave us hurrying and rushed. If you overestimate rather than underestimate the time it takes, it will help you avoid the stress that rushing creates.

2. Do not put off until tomorrow what needs to be done today. Procrastination is a thief of time and productivity. Often our tendency is to put off what we do not enjoy doing even though it will inevitably have to be done. Enjoy the additional peace when it's no longer looming over you. Procrastination is also a thief of healthy margin and peace because it makes ordinary tasks fall into the category of urgent.

3. Disconnect from social media and reconnect with peace, family, and God. I have learned to power down my devices to create a reprieve from the constant ding, and expectations for response. I'm guilty of setting my phone down for hours and forgetting to check it which has occasionally gotten me in trouble with my family, but balance and moderation are what we're aiming for.

4. Go for a walk, play a game, or read an inspirational book. These moments are blessings for the body and soul. Exercise is another wonderful way to decompress and release stress and anxiety. Anything that will help set you on a healthier path for your body, soul, and spirit should be part of your margin.

5. Create daily lists to maintain focus on your priorities. I usually text myself the night before to remind myself of the important items on my agenda for the next day. This helps protect my time and energy from distractions that can divert my attention, leading to stress when tasks are left undone. Remember to make a manageable to do list that doesn't leave you feeling burdened, and keep you from spending quality time with your loved ones.

6. Obey the Creator. "Remember the Sabbath day, to keep it holy. Six days you shall labor, and do all your work, but the seventh day is a Sabbath to the Lord your God. On it you shall not do any work, you, or your son, or your daughter, your male servant, or your female servant, or your livestock, or the sojourner who is within your gates. For in six days the Lord made heaven and earth, the sea, and all that is in them, and rested on the seventh day. Therefore, **the Lord blessed the Sabbath day** and made it holy" (Exodus 20:8-11, ESV).

If God rested, we need to rest. Don't crowd every day with activity and responsibility. Make one day per week a necessary day of leisure, rest, and recuperation. When we honor the Lord with our obedience in stewarding our time and resources, He has a miraculous way of making the rest of our time and resources more productive and efficient.

Oh, how I wish my desire for change would have created an overnight success story. But the truth is, this has taken years filled with hits and misses. Pain, frustration, tears, and stress have consumed my days as a mother and wife. As I share the insights the Lord has graciously revealed to me along the way, I pray you'll feel the Lord extending the same invitation to you to listen and learn His ways.

Perhaps you're not wrestling with inner hostility poised to attack the next person needing something from you. Maybe you're just weighed down with fatigue, uncertain of what to do about it. Dear friend, take heart. The Lord sees, cares, and stands ready to unshackle your weary, over-burdened heart.

"Come to me, all you who are weary and burdened, and I will give you rest. Take my yoke upon you and learn from me, for I am gentle and humble in heart, and you will find rest for your souls. For my yoke is easy and my burden is light" (Matthew 11:28-30, NIV).

If I can help you avoid a day of unnecessary wear and tear by implementing even one tip the Lord has shown me, this chapter will be worth it. Here's a peek into what my older self would sit down and share with my younger self moving forward:

1. No is not a bad word! Do not feel guilty if you have to say no to some commitments to make some space for your mental, physical, and spiritual health. Your no today could make room for a more important yes tomorrow.

2. Life's demands can indeed be overwhelming but do not let the urgent consume the important. There will always be more work than time so learn the freedom that prioritizing creates. When something lesser begins to demand more, go back to number 1.

3. Don't let life pass you by in a blur of disappointment. Unrealistic expectations can steal joy and beauty from your everyday life. Stop, count your blessings, and take some time to actually enjoy them.

4. Live gratefully! Learn to appreciate what you have right now.

5. Live in the present. Wherever you're at, be ALL there. Live more focused, with the least number of distractions, including your cell phone, especially when you are with people you love. Let them know you love them enough to be fully present.

6. Love your people with kindness and compassion and forgive them for their flaws. Listen more than talk, love more than fear, care more than judge.

7. Live more unguarded and braver. It may be risky and painful, but it will also be empowering. Life is a journey that shows us both beauty and brokenness, but every day is a gift to be cherished. Life is too short to waste precious time being afraid.

Lie: Margin is for the weak and incapable.
Truth:

Margin is for the wise. It embodies the principles in the Word of God. The Creator of Heaven and Earth has given us His counsel to be at our best. To heed His advice is like a beautiful dancer twirling graciously in the ballroom of life; to ignore it would be a clumsy stumble in our existence.

"It is useless for you to work so hard from early morning until late at night, anxiously working for food to eat; for God gives rest to his loved ones" (Psalm 127:2, NLT).

"He makes me lie down in green pastures. He leads me beside still waters. He restores my soul" (Psalm 23:2-3a, ESV).

"So then, there remains a Sabbath rest for the people of God, for whoever has entered God's rest has also rested from his works as God did from his" (Hebrews 4:9-10, ESV).

"So let us do our best to enter that rest. But if we disobey God, as the people of Israel did, we will fall" (Hebrews 4:11, NLT).

Embracing a sabbath should be a command that is simple to implement yet is often overlooked. Refusing to rest willingly may lead to forced breaks later due to illness, mental breakdown, or fractured relationships. Let's be proactive: savor life's fullness by taking intentional sabbaths. Rest, rejuvenate, and relish your life. You only get one life to live, so live it well.

"Jesus said to them, 'The Sabbath was made to meet the needs of people, and not people to meet the requirements of the Sabbath'" (Mark 2:27, NIV).

Closing prayer:

Lord, sometimes I find it difficult to set healthy margins in my life. I often push myself too hard and need Your help to better manage my time, energy, and resources. I'm so used to constant activity that pausing feels strange. I know Your ways are what's best for me, but I need Your help to put them into practice for my physical, emotional, and spiritual well-being. Amen.

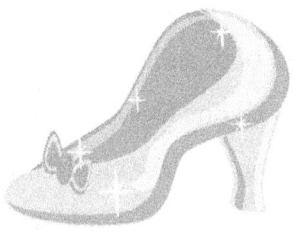

Chapter 11

Contentment in the Most Unlikely Place

"...I have learned to be content whatever the circumstances" (Philippians 4:11, NIV).

I wish I could say the above scripture has been my life verse, but I'd be lying! True contentment has been a distant friend I have longed to visit but often failed to find. The day my dad turned 40, I was 14 years old and remember seeing the words "Lordy, Lordy, Pastor's 40" written across our Astro minivan!

The black balloons, Over the Hill pictures and streamers were a visual reminder of how old my dad was. There were some wrinkles, grey hair, a dad bod, and corny jokes that made me think my dad was living with one foot in the grave. I never imagined that day would ever show up for me. In my adolescent mind, 40 defined old, and I was sure Jesus would return before I arrived at that season.

As you can imagine, Jesus did not show up before my 40th birthday, and I'm comfortably past that mile marker now. I wake up and see the same signs of aging I was sure was only one birthday away from seeing Jesus. I laugh now at how young 40 actually is and love the freedom that has emerged with this age.

I have spent much of my life wrestling with perfectionism that has stolen precious moments I should have been enjoying. I believed there was a perfect season and reality I could reach if I just worked hard enough for it. My belief turned out to be a lie and a waste of precious time. My misguided idealism drained my contentment. Time, energy, and effort were wasted on things that:

1. Were unrealistic.
2. Did not matter, in light of the BIG picture.
3. Were going to change no matter how hard I tried to keep them the same.

Cosmetic, pharmaceutical, and fitness companies everywhere are marketing to aging women, promising to help them regain their youth in a bottle. "Try free for 30 days, satisfaction guaranteed or your money back" is their slogan. It all sounds wonderful, so wonderful, in fact, that these companies make billions of dollars targeting a woman's vulnerabilities. Our culture feeds us never-ending lies that youth and beauty are requirements necessary for happiness in this life. We believe our worth will be greater, and our status will be elevated. Even though we know it's ridiculous, we still buy the lies and the products to try and keep what can't be kept.

"Charm is deceptive, and beauty is fleeting; but a woman who fears the Lord is to be praised" (Proverbs 31:30, NIV).

My life has been evolving moment by moment, mistake after mistake, regret after regret, even success after success. God is a God of seasons; we can see the reality of this in the creation all around us. Yet, as a woman, wife, and mom, I have often resisted life's natural progression, trying to manage the process to arrive at my perfect destination, which, in reality, was a fantasy and futile pursuit.

From an early age, I can remember wanting to be someone, somewhere, or have something different. As a child, I'd dream about being a teenager; as a teenager, I longed for adulthood; as a single adult, I longed to be married; as a married woman, I longed to be a parent; as a full-time parent, I longed for empty nesting. I was always longing for the next, thinking something different would bring me the happiness and contentment

I desired. The term used to describe this yearning is *sehnsucht*. C.S. Lewis described *sehnsucht* as an inconsolable longing for we know not what. He concluded that these experiences of longing are valuable only as a pointer to something other and outer. They are meant to be signposts pointing us to our Creator.

My yearning for that elusive "something" caused me to seek and find that the only source of true joy in life is Jesus. When I finally ran to my Heavenly Father with my desires, He helped me lay down my yearning and yield—yield to the beautiful reality that was sitting right in front of me.

> *He opened my eyes to see that looking for the next keeps me from fully embracing and enjoying the now.*

The more we struggle to change our seasons, or even keep a season beyond its expiration, the more discontented and frustrated we will become.

I missed many moments in my active parenting days when I should have just sat, listened, and laughed more. I was so busy rushing to the next thing that I missed time to connect and be content. When my youngest was finishing her first year in college we planned a vacation where all of the girls were able to come. We had a lovely time. One particular morning, I asked the girls to join me for breakfast and coffee. I felt it was time to finally share parts of my story that I had never shared with any of them. With my notes in hand and a heart of vulnerability, I opened up and to my surprise, they did too.

I heard stories from their childhood that I never knew, stories that made me cry and laugh but, most of all, made me feel sorry — sorry that I didn't know. Was it because I was too busy doing and pushing ahead? I'm not sure, and I can't go back, but I'm so glad I can move forward with a heart of understanding and grace that wouldn't have come if I hadn't taken the time to just sit in the moment. I came across a quote that I've learned is essential for living our best life and it goes like this: "Wherever you are, be all there."

I'm now a middle-aged woman with wrinkles, grey hair, sagging skin, extra weight in my mid-section, and hot flashes that are amazing—I mean, annoying. This is one season I never longed for or dreamed would become a reality, yet here I sit, and I can honestly say, "It's good! I'm good!" Now, in my 50s, I no longer look like I did in my 20s; I look better! Not because my skin is tight or my size 4 jeans still fit, not because my hair is full and shiny, or because my energy is unstoppable, but because I finally see the beauty from years of time-tested experience and wisdom surfacing. Like fine wine, I have become better with age. Things that used to ruffle my feathers are now less burdensome. I'm enjoying life more, relationships more, family more, and, of course, my Jesus more.

Perspectives have shifted, wisdom has grown, and life is so much sweeter! There are virtues at this stage in life I never had in my youth. There's a newfound peace, patience, and purpose. Priorities have also shifted. I recognize that there are specific things and people God has assigned me to, as part of His plan. I don't have to do everything that comes across my path, neither do I need to work at impressing others for them to like me.

I understand that I may not matter to most people, but I truly matter to some, and it's those few who are my life's assignment and will be my legacy. Recognizing this prevents me from wasting any more time trying to influence others' opinions of me. I've learned to prioritize the relationships that matter and stop wasting precious time with people who only tolerate me rather than appreciate me. Those who appreciate you will see your value and will be open to receiving you as a gift in their life. They will be the ones on whom you'll have the most significant impact.

Another nugget of gold I've mined through experience is to stop wasting time on activities I'm not good at and do not like. It's not my gift! This barometer has helped me clarify my purpose, focus my energy, and preserve my sanity. In part, it is what inspired me to write this book to highlight the greatness of a God who strategically works in the lives of His children through their unique giftedness. The challenges I've faced have helped build a faith that knows God's purpose and timing are always best!

It's not age that has made life better; it's been the process, seasons of submission, and learning along the way. The process will either make us seasoned and better or battered and bitter. Much of our life is about the choices we make throughout our journey.

> *We don't always get to choose what we go through, but we can choose how we go through it. We are not mindless participants in life's circumstances.*

Circumstances, both good and bad, can produce wisdom, strength, and even hope in us. Every slammed door, crushed dream, broken promise, and tear-drenched pillow can be used, by our Heavenly Father, to mold and make us into a more beautiful version of ourselves.

"For our present troubles are small and won't last very long. Yet they produce for us a glory that vastly outweighs them and will last forever" (2 Corinthians 4:17, NLT).

It is our Creator's joy to fix broken things and repurpose battered things. The question for us is, will we let Him? If life is all about choices, we must choose to surrender in the hard moments allowing what we go through to produce what God has intended. The pressure and harshness of the elements around us will either produce a diamond or coal; we get to choose.

"And we know that God causes everything to work together for the good of those who love God and are called according to his purpose for them" (Romans 8:28, NLT).

I've faced some hard moments in life; some still bring tears to my eyes, but many of those tears are now from laughter rather than sorrow. The experience I'm about to share illustrates this perfectly. In an earlier season of my life, this would have crushed me with embarrassment, but now I find it quite funny and a valuable lesson I can share with others.

As one of the worship leaders at our church, I was leading a song I really enjoyed, and in my zeal, I rolled an ankle and fell. Oh honey, this was not just any fall; it was a fall of epic proportions where my legs flew out in front of me and proceeded straight into the air! It was not graceful in the least! Thankfully, I was wearing pants! I didn't miss a beat; I got up; kept singing and successfully finished the entire worship set.

Later that day, my daughter asked, "Mom, how in the world did you keep singing like nothing happened?" I had to admit that when I was her age (early 20s), something like this would have embarrassed me so badly that I probably would have started crying and walked off the stage. The sheer humiliation of having people see my ungraceful fall would have sent me reeling. I would have wanted to hide and not return to the stage for a very long time, but not today. What's changed? Me!

I'm no longer worried about what others might think of me. A deeper sense of contentment and humility has developed through life's experiences and God's grace. This season, which I once feared would be my end, has actually been just the beginning. I've finally reached a place where I understand what is important. I know that I am fully loved and accepted, and this realization has set me free! I don't have to perform to earn anyone else's acceptance because I already have the complete love and endorsement of my Creator. He adores me, and sister, He adores you too!

Please, stop lamenting over things you cannot change. Stop wasting precious time trying to manufacture something only God can produce. If something needs to change, trust God's wisdom and timing.

> *Don't keep wishing yourself into another season when God wants to produce something in this season that can't be produced in the next.*

Don't try to outrun the details. Yield and embrace the moment because you'll never get a chance to live it again. His timing and work in us is perfect; when He's done, it will never leave you lacking.

Lie: I'll be happier when...
Truth:

"He has made everything beautiful and appropriate in its time. He has also planted eternity [a sense of divine purpose] in the human heart [a mysterious longing which nothing under the sun can satisfy, except God]—yet man cannot find out (comprehend, grasp) what God has done (His overall plan) from the beginning to the end" (Ecclesiastes 3:11, Amp).

Before you move on, take a few moments to sit in this truth. Fully embrace the fact that God unapologetically loves you. He has preserved you, helped you survive, and has a great plan He is working in you. Even if that plan is not fully realized or developed, choose to grow through each season. Sit back, rest, and enjoy the process because who you are today is wiser and stronger than yesterday, and who you'll be tomorrow will be stronger and wiser than today as you yield to His plan for your life.

Closing prayer:

Thank you, Father, for all of the blessings you've poured into my life. Please help me to find joy in each moment you graciously allow me to experience. May the beauty of this season take my breath away and remind me to cherish the now instead of pushing toward what's next. I am grateful for each new day and ask for Your help to live fully in the present with enjoyment and a sense of purpose. Amen.

Chapter 12

Acceptance and Trust

In the same way, the sun never grows weary of shining, nor a stream flowing, it is God's nature to keep His promises. ~ Charles Spurgeon

Don't you just love a good story? Romance, intrigue, action, mystery, comedy, I love them all, but I have to admit the Cinderella story is one of my favorites. I have watched many versions of this classic and still enjoy the predictable storyline. Why? Because of the ending. There's not only justice, but true love emerges out of the wreckage. Isn't that what we all long for, a life where beauty arises from ashes? Another reason I enjoy this classic is because of the great love and bond depicted between Cinderella and her father, especially after the death of her mother. Cinderella greatly loved and respected her daddy. She drew her sense of strength and stability from his presence in her life. Even after his absence, he was still influencing the woman she became. I can relate to Cinderella also having a great father in my life. I was able to reap the rewards of his protection as he valiantly watched over and cared for his family. His influence is also still shaping my life.

Even with the investment of a good Father, I still lived with significant deficits in my soul, which kept me striving for the affirmation and love of others to fill the holes. Though I grew up knowing God loved me, I wrestled with self-doubt. I continued placing pressure on others to fill what was lacking. I even stepped into marriage with a fantasy mindset that my husband would become my prince charming and fix all of my insecurities. If you're married, you're probably laughing right now because we all know that dear person we married came into the relationship with their own set of fears, failures, and insecurities. They probably had some expectations of their own that you would be the missing piece to their puzzle for wholeness.

I'll share the actual reality I was living in my marriage but, let me start with this disclaimer: I have one of the greatest husbands a woman could ask for. He's been a wonderful father to our girls, a loyal friend, a faithful husband, and companion, but he also had deep wounds he was wading through. They affected me, and my wounds affected him. Our wounds began to show up very early in our marriage, in fact, on the honeymoon! It's quite a laughable story now, but in that moment, it was disastrous! So, let me spill the tea.

I'm not a great sports enthusiast, but my husband is. He played sports all throughout high school and college. To say the least, he was competitive and did not like to lose! Coming from a very non-athletic, competitive background, I didn't understand how important winning was to him and how losing (especially to a girl) was a blow to his ego. This is where the funny begins…we were on our honeymoon at a beautiful resort, enjoying the evening outdoors around a very elaborate pool deck surrounded by ping pong tables and other activities. Knowing he enjoys games, we decided to play some table tennis, and lo and behold, I started to win. I could sense his frustration the more we played, so in my great wisdom, I decided to stop playing. I laid my paddle down and began to walk away. The next thing I knew, he grabbed my ponytail and pulled me toward the table to finish the game. "We're not done." He exclaimed. I was completely dumbfounded and replied, "Yes, we are!" In shock I ran away and arrived at the hotel room before he did. I locked myself inside and refused to let him in. I was devastated thinking I had just married an abuser! It took a couple of hours of repenting and crying, in the hallway, before I decided to open the door and let him in. Thankfully, this occurrence was the first and last time my husband ever did anything like that. It's a funny story we often share with other couples about how NOT to manage conflict in marriage.

Through years of personal growth and submission to the Holy Spirit in our lives, we have realized it was fear, insecurities, and other deficits that caused us to react in such ways. I feared anyone being angry at me, not liking me and eventually abandoning me. He also had a deep-rooted fear of looking like a failure, which caused him to react in anger. Many times, our fears and responses to those fears are imprinted on us as children. Whether intentional or unintentional, our families of origin often cause wounds that leave us oozing pain unto others. Often, we don't even recognize some of our core fears that have developed over the years. It's not until we are repeating cycles, we can't seem to exit, that we begin to recognize our own deficits. When we become self-aware and intentional to change, the Holy Spirit is waiting to step in and work on us, healing our souls from the inside out when we finally ask.

As I began my journey toward wholeness, I remember hearing a podcast where the speaker asked, "Is there anything in your life that causes an immediate reaction? If so, what? Now ask yourself, why." I started to see that every time my husband came across angry or sharp it would immediately cause me to react. Those core fears of having someone angry at me, not being liked, and eventually abandoning me would creep in, so I'd put up walls to defend my heart. Instead of reacting verbally, I'd stone-wall and walk away, which is equally harmful. It left him feeling unheard as if I didn't value him or his feelings; that triggered his fear of failure. It kept us on a crazy cycle of insult and injury for a very long time.

In my quest for answers, I reached out to a number of women and asked them to share some of their core fears and needs. I wanted to see if there was a common thread in what I was dealing with. What I found just confirmed some research I had previously read. Most women have two very basic needs: 1. to be cherished and have someone value them despite their flaws. 2. to be protected and feel secure without fear of abandonment.

There's no doubt that we feel safer, better adjusted, and more equipped to succeed when we come from a strong, stable family of origin built on a foundation of love, acceptance, and protection. Unfortunately, we will still be confronted with doubts and fears. It's even greater in families that are fractured and, at best, surviving but not thriving. We have an epidemic of absentee fathers and mothers who choose selfish ambitions, personal pleasures, or financial successes over nurturing their own child/children, leaving emotional wreckage in the wake.

Many of you reading this did not/do not have a healthy relationship with your parents. Because of it, you are still bearing the emotional scars and fighting the insecurities that were created. In our current generation, living in a family without a father's presence is more common than with a father's presence. As sad as this is, there's good news. We do not have to continually live and bear the emotional wounds an absent father/parent has left.

We have a Heavenly Father who has not only invited us into His family but has also provided for us healing from every hurt and insecurity we have ever experienced. He has borne it all on Himself at the cross so we can live in hope. "He himself bore our sins in his body on the tree, that we might die to sin and live to righteousness. **By his wounds you have been healed**" (1 Peter 2:24, ESV).

"You have not received a spirit that makes you fearful slaves. Instead, you received God's Spirit when He adopted you as His own children. Now we call Him Abba Father (Daddy)" (Romans 8:15, NLT).

"Blessed be the God and Father of our Lord Jesus Christ! According to His great mercy, He has caused us to be born again to a living hope through the resurrection of Jesus Christ from the dead" (I Peter 1:3, ESV).

These scriptures are wonderful reminders of a very real relationship and gift of love we've been given; but it's not an automatic life-giving experience. We must also contribute to this relationship before we will experience it in its fullness. The contributions we need to bring to the table are *acceptance* and *trust*.

Let me present this in a word picture that may be a little easier to understand. In college, I met a young man who was eager to get to know me. He started hanging out with my circle of friends; showing up at places I frequented and began doing special things to attract my attention. Even after I initially declined his invitation to go out with him, he continued to try and woo my affections. This so reminds me of God's relentless pursuit of those He loves, even when we reject Him, He continues to love us so that one day we will open our hearts to Him.

Now, back to my story, after seeing him more frequently and getting to know him better, I began to enjoy his company and eventually ACCEPTED his invitation to go out on an actual date. My acceptance of his invitation set me up to know him better; and knowing him better established a TRUST in him that eventually led to marriage. Do you see how acceptance and trust was left up to me? The same is true in our relationship with our Heavenly Father. He has a proven, dependable track record that is selfless and giving, but we will never fully understand the depth of that selfless love until we first accept His invitation to "Taste and see that the Lord is Good; Oh, the joys of those who take refuge in Him" (Psalm 34:8, NLT). Once we accept that invitation and get to know Him, trust will follow. With that trust, we will grow comfortable placing our hope, security and dreams, both past and present, in Him because He is so faithful and generous with His great love.

> *Our soul is like a vacuum cleaner that ravenously sucks up everything it comes in contact with, whether it's something that adds value to our lives or not.*

God created our soul with a deep longing and appetite for Him. Because our emotions often drive our appetites, we must make sure our souls stay healthy. We have to stop running to sources that leave us longing, whether it be food we run to for comfort, people for affirmation, success for status, or a plethora of other things. When our appetites draw us away from the source of life, it will cause emotional, relational, and spiritual deprivation. Filling our souls with the wrong things leaves us thirstier and more deprived than before. We must intentionally draw our comfort and refreshment from the only true source of life, Jesus. Again, the more we get to know Him by spending time in His sweet presence, the easier it is to trust Him and surrender our pain, brokenness, disappointment, and fear. Only then will He be able to fill our souls with real refreshment. "Jesus answered, 'Everyone who drinks this water will soon become thirsty again, but those who drink the water I give will never be thirsty again. It becomes a fresh, bubbling spring within them, giving them eternal life" (John 4:13-14, NLT).

Daily maintenance is imperative to keep our soul free of debris. This includes daily seeking His truth, which purges deception, contamination, and lies that the enemy would love for us to believe. Truth (God's Word) is the only thing that can defeat deception, and light is the only thing that can dispel darkness, so let's pursue what will nourish us rather than deplete us. "I lift up my hands to you in prayer. I thirst for you as parched land thirsts for rain" Psalm 143:6 (NLT).

A flowing spring within us will help us function as active contributors in this life, not just parched takers. My sincere hope for each of us is that we develop a deeper understanding of Jesus, not merely through what we've heard, but by forming our own personal connection. May this relationship encourage us to *accept* Truth and *trust* Him more every day.

Closing prayer:

Jesus, my soul is thirsty, and sometimes I'm guilty of filling it with things that contaminate me. Please forgive me and heal my broken heart. Help me fill my life with what adds value and nourishment—You. Draw me close to You as I seek to know and serve You. Help me understand Your Word and the depth of Your amazing love for me. Thank You for never giving up on me. Amen.

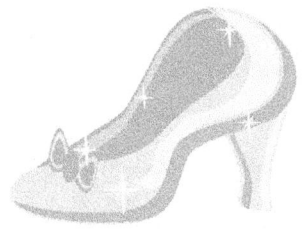

Chapter 13
Sisters Are Necessary

Girls may find themselves competing, but Real Sisters rise together. Girls may tear each other down, but Real Sisters lift each other up. Girls may compare, but Real Sisters champion one another. ~ Author Unknown

I was over the moon! My first "official" boyfriend was coming over – he was the first one my parents knew about, and I wanted everything to be perfect – hair styled, makeup on, house clean – check! My fifteen-year-old self was determined not to mess up this opportunity to date an older man. He was a seventeen-year-old senior, popular, and had his own car. This was the dream!

He showed up and my dad, seizing the moment, decided to kick things off with "the talk." He laid out his fatherly expectations regarding our "friendship," Phew! We survived that! The evening continued with some family games and laughter. I thought everything was going wonderfully until we walked outside on the porch. I was anticipating a hug before he left, but instead, he dropped a bomb I was not expecting. "Lynette, you're an awesome girl, but I think we should just be friends. To be honest, I really like ... (he named one of my best friends) ... more." "What?!" I burst out. "You just met her! You don't even know her!" I began to question him, but the conversation ended abruptly, and he left, leaving me with a broken heart.

Assumptions were running hot! I was hurt but not by him. I was mad at her! How could she do this to me? She knew how much I liked him. She must have been flirting with him behind my back! This is the second boyfriend she's stolen from me. What a great friend she is! I reasoned. Thankfully my fifteen-year-old-self moved on quickly and we continued our friendship. We're still friends today.

I was recently on vacation with my husband, staying in a cute beach town on the Gulf of America. I was walking the beach one afternoon when I stumbled across a hopeless crab being battered by the waves that kept washing ashore and pushing the crab further unto the sand. Every time the wave subsided, he'd try for the water only to be pushed back again and again by another wave. Finally, after watching this repeated occurrence, I came to his rescue. It reminded me of what can happen to us when we've been battered by hurt, misunderstanding, or accusations that have left us feeling betrayed. Betrayal, disappointment and pain caused by others can result in feelings of mistrust causing us to view everyone through a tainted lens if we don't forgive and let it go. Unmanaged pain can be a dangerous place to remain because if left alone, we're vulnerable and become easy prey to bitterness leaving us reluctant to trust others again.

"The Lord God said, "It is not good for man to be alone...." Genesis 2:18 (NIV). God has created us for community and a sense of belonging. While many discover this connection with their families and friends, others choose to sit on the sidelines with a guarded heart never fully open to the possibilities of what true sisterhood could bring. God's design is intentional, and since He's the Creator, He knows what essential elements will nurture and empower us the most. I realize that finding good people to trek with us through the ups and downs of life isn't easy, and fear can keep us from letting anyone too close. But, it will only be to our advantage to pursue what our Creator has ordained for our betterment. Maybe you worry the effort won't be worth the return. What if they hurt me?

> *Hurt is always a possibility when we open our hearts, but I've come to realize feeling hurt is better than being numb and feeling nothing at all.*

Though it may be challenging to build meaningful connections, it is so worthwhile. Despite difficulty, I have seen how good relationships help us fulfill God's purposes and plans for our lives. While researching for this book, I found that many women yearn for at least one close genuine friend. They desire someone who will lend an attentive ear, a caring shoulder to cry on and provide honest feedback, but instead, they settle for surface friendships rather than investing to build a life-giving sisterhood that inspires, motivates, and challenges them to be better.

Many relationships start with promise but unravel due to unrealistic expectations and other negative patterns. Jealousy, competition, and gossip, has been an ebb and flow I've often witnessed between "friends." The feeling of distrust that follows when there's repeated hurt can cause us to retreat from relationships in order to protect our heart and reputation. Ladies, why do we do this to one another, making authentic sisterhood a difficult thing to achieve? I know the pain, I've been there; I've also felt the pressure to meet others' expectations. It has often left me drained and hurt halting my desire to pursue and nurture strong sister connections. If we're keeping it real, there are circumstances and seasons in all of our lives when additional relational investments are near impossible. And that's okay as long as that season doesn't become a sanctuary of isolation that you refuse to leave.

Parenting my young daughters was one of those seasons in my life. I had three girls in four years and was thrilled when I could just carve out enough time to shower. I had little time to invest in any close connections outside of my immediate family. Thankfully, I had a couple of sisters who kept me sane and grounded even when I couldn't reciprocate. True sisters see and understand those seasons in our lives. Instead of being hurt, jealous or offended by your lack of investment they know when to jump in to help, call to talk, and pray for your strength to persevere.

In a previous chapter, I mentioned the Lioness Arising Bible study by Lisa Bevere. I'm going to share the same story but with a different perspective. She painted a vivid picture that is particularly relevant in this chapter as we discuss the importance of healthy relationships. The story is about three lions that were raised in captivity. When they were old enough to survive independently, the boundaries that had once confined them were removed in hopes that they would reconnect with the wild. Barriers were lifted and they were introduced to new territory, yet these lions refused to venture beyond the line that had once been their boundary. They had become so comfortable, and complacent in their captivity that it required drastic measures from the keepers of the habitat to encourage them to cross their invisible confinement. They eventually stopped feeding the lions; instead, they killed a deer and placed it downwind, hoping the hunger would urge them beyond their invisible borders. The lions' hunger finally became greater than their hesitancy, and they journeyed into the unknown.

What is so beautiful about all of this is the rest of the story:

Only two dared to explore, leaving one still back in captivity. They instinctively knew she wouldn't survive without food, so they dragged the kill all the way back to provide the strength and nourishment the remaining lion needed to live. This is a picture of true sisterhood, yet in reality many relationships are founded on what we can get rather than what we can give. Selfishness always hinders the growth of healthy relationships. In fact, it is one of the primary reasons why many relationships fail.

> *A healthy relationship is like a mirror that reflects the worst of who we are while offering a safe space to help us develop into the best of who we can become.*

I hate to admit it, but when I got married, I was incredibly selfish. My understanding of marriage focused more on how much my spouse should give rather than on what I needed to contribute. With two selfish individuals merging into this new relationship called marriage, we clashed time and time again—one strong will against the other, each of us wanting our own way. In fairness, my husband compromised more than I did just to keep the peace. My whining and manipulation bent his will more than his attempts to bend mine. We've come a long way from those chaotic beginnings, and I'm so thankful that God has used my marriage as a refining tool. *What if marriage is meant to make us more holy not just more happy? ~ Gary Thomas.* This is a great quote to ponder, but it extends beyond marriage, as God also uses other relationships as a refining tool.

Sisters can have a significant impact on our emotional and spiritual growth. James stated that we must, "Confess our sins to each other and pray for each other so that we may be healed" (James 5:16, NIV). The Bible instructs us to cultivate friendships where we can confess our sins and be able to trust that those to whom we confess will not judge us but will support us, hold us accountable, and pray for our healing.

> *God's idea for us to live in community was not just to avoid loneliness, but to assist each other in healing and development.*

Sisterhood is meant to be a blessing to help us on our spiritual journey.

"A friend loves at all times, and a brother is born for adversity" (Proverbs 17:17, ESV).

Let me just replace the word "brother" with "sister" in this text, and you'll understand another reason why having a good sister is so important. We will all experience adversity at some point in life, but adversity won't break us if we have a strong support system. It is much easier to face pain and difficulty when the burden is shared with others who are willing to help carry the load.

"Bear one another's burdens and so fulfill the law of Christ" (Galatians 6:2, ESV).

Being a sister that will help carry another's burdens is a Biblical mandate meant to assist us in our most difficult moments. We need each other, so please don't just sit idly by hoping for a sister to come your way without first choosing to be a sister yourself. If we choose to love more deeply during both the manicured and messy moments of life, it will make living more manageable and enjoyable for all involved.

Let's make it our mission to be women who invest in developing a beautiful culture for sisterhood to thrive by being women who:

1. Create a safe space for vulnerability — one of the most wonderful aspects of sisterhood is that we can truly let our

guards down with other women. As sisters we shouldn't have to hide our imperfections or pretend we have it all together; instead, we should be the safest place for others to be vulnerable and provide support for life's ups and downs.

"Above all, keep loving one another earnestly, since love covers a multitude of sins. Show hospitality to one another without grumbling. As each has received a gift, use it to serve one another, as good stewards of God's varied grace" (1 Peter 4;8-10, ESV).

2. Share our stories with others — research shows that sharing our story, especially with those who've faced similar challenges, can help us heal more quickly from trauma than facing it alone. Sharing our stories can also become a source of encouragement for others facing the same challenges. It reminds us that we're never alone in our journey.

"Oil and perfume make the heart glad, and the sweetness of a friend comes from his earnest counsel" (Proverbs 27:9, ESV).

3. Encourage others — as women, we often face negative messages about our bodies, achievements, and worth, however being surrounded by supportive women who will celebrate one another's strengths and accomplishments can help us counteract these harmful messages. When we lift each other up, we create a beautiful space that enhances everyone's worth. Encouragement is the healthiest environment for people to flourish.

"Therefore encourage one another and build one another up, just as you are doing" (1 Thessalonians 5:11, ESV).

4. Inspire growth and personal development — create an environment that encourages others to dream, learn and grow. Having a network of supportive sisters is invaluable for broadening our horizons. With sisters cheering us on, we gain the confidence to make our goals a reality. Sisterhood isn't just about uplifting ourselves; it's also about lifting up those around us so they will succeed. Authentic sisterhood will take time and effort to be present and purposeful, but the investment will yield beautiful possibilities.
"And let us consider how to stir up one another to love and good works, not neglecting to meet together, as is the habit of some, but encouraging one another..." (Hebrews 10:24-25a, ESV).

Lie: I don't need any sisters.
Truth:
This bond is an essential source of strength and resilience for all of us. Both research and the Word of God confirm this truth. No matter what sisterhood looks like in your own life, whether you have sisters in close proximity, sisters that rely on technology to stay connected, or you have life-long friends that even when separated by large quantities of time can reconnect and pick right back up where you left off ... whatever it looks

like … keep investing in it. If you are one who's missing out, don't stop looking; don't stop trying. Ask the Lord to help you find another woman or group of women to share life with. Be intentional to look for ways to cultivate deeper connections. Sisterhood is too important to be passive about so, let's seek real sisterhood and strive to embody it ourselves.

"Treat people the same way you want them to treat you" (Luke 6:31, NASB).

Closing prayer:

Lord, thank you for the friends and family You have placed in my life. Help me to love them with intention. I want to extend genuine friendship to others and be a safe place for them to land. Remove jealousy, toxic comparison, and any other hindrance to healthy friendships. Thank You for enabling me to cultivate authentic sisterhood and fulfill Your purpose for relationships in my life. Amen.

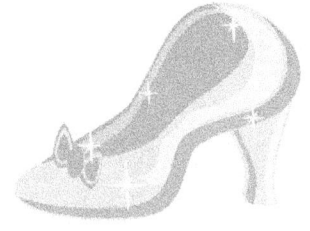

Chapter 14
Now A Princess

"To be a princess you have to believe that you ARE a princess." ~ Mia (Princess Diaries)

I recently heard a story about the Queen of England. She was invited to an elaborate fundraising gala with heads of states, famous athletes, movie stars, and other royalty. Many were already present when she arrived. As she entered the room, she commanded the attention of every famous onlooker present. The aura she brought with her was palatable esteem and honor. When she stepped into the room her head was held high, her posture erect, her eyes were bright and observant, and the grace with which she walked caused others to bow their head in her direction. As I listened to this story from one who was present, I marveled at his description of her. Her entrance so captivated him that I wondered if he even saw anyone else in the room.

She wasn't the prettiest, youngest, most successful, talented, fit, or intelligent, but when she walked into that room it didn't matter. She was the queen, and she knew who she was. Her poise, confidence, and grace commanded everyone's attention, as it should. Friend, this may seem like a strange finale to this book, but let me assure you, God has a message that I do NOT want you to miss.

"For you did not receive the spirit of slavery to fall back into fear, but you have received the Spirit of adoption as sons (and daughters), by whom we cry, 'Abba, Father" (Romans 8:15, ESV).

"And since we are His children, we are His heirs. In fact, together with Christ we are heirs of God's glory..." (Romans 8:17, NLT).

I want to point out a few significant truths from the above scriptures. If you can accept it as truth, it will change the view you have of yourself and how others will perceive you going forward!

1. Because THE KING has adopted you, it's made your past

irrelevant. It does not matter if you come from a background of abandonment, poverty, shame, addiction, abuse, or any other adjective; your past does NOT define your future nor current status of being loved and accepted. I've stated it numerous times throughout this book, but it is so true: God's love is not based on us; it's just graciously placed on us. Regardless of any weakness or flaw in your past or present, God loves you and has chosen you for His family. Your life of fear and rejection is over; you are now adopted by the King.

2. Because you are a child of the King that makes you a princess! Maybe you look at yourself and think, I'm not very pretty, smart, talented, or successful, but it does not matter, nor does it change the fact that you are eternally loved! It's not based on your image or performance but on **His** perfect ability to love. "But God showed His great love for us by sending Christ to die for us while we were still sinners" (Romans 5:8, NLT).

God does not wait for us to get our act together to bestow His love and acceptance on us. He saw your incredible need, so He extravagantly stepped in to meet the greatest need you and I would ever have… LOVE. To be fully loved and accepted despite our imperfections is life-changing when we genuinely understand this! "Greater love has no one than this: to lay down one's life for one's friends" (John 15:13, NIV).

3. As a child of the King, you are *the heir* to His great fortunes. You should never again be regarded as an orphan, pauper, or misfit. You are royalty, making you an heiress to the greatest treasures ever given to mankind.

Beyond the promises of Christ's rewards in Heaven as mentioned in the following scriptures:

"God blesses those who patiently endure testing and temptation. Afterward, they will receive the crown of life that God has promised to those who love him" (James 1:12, NLT).

"Yet what we suffer now is nothing compared to the glory he will reveal to us later" (Romans 8:18, NLT).

"Look, I am coming soon! My reward is with me, and I will give to each person according to what they have done" (Revelation 22:12, NIV).

We also have promises of great treasure here on earth that money could never buy:

1. We have a personal relationship with the Creator. "So now we can rejoice in our wonderful new relationship with God because our Lord Jesus Christ has made us friends of God" (Romans 5:11, NLT).

2. We have the fruits of His Spirit. "But the Holy Spirit produces this kind of fruit in our lives: love, joy, peace, patience,

kindness, goodness, faithfulness, gentleness, and self-control. There is no law against these things" (Galatians 5:22–23, NLT).

3. We have been given the resources to overcome every attack of the enemy. "Submit therefore to God. Resist the devil and he will flee from you. Draw near to God and He will draw near to you..." James 4:7-8 (NASB).
"Finally, be strong in the Lord and in the strength of His might. Put on the full armor of God, so that you will be able to stand firm against the schemes of the devil. For our struggle is not against flesh and blood, but against the rulers, against the powers, against the world forces of this darkness, against the spiritual forces of wickedness in the heavenly places" (Ephesians 6:10–17, NASB).

We are not mere victims or survivors in this life; we are royal heirs of the King. It's time to believe it!

> *Stand tall, lift your head, and step confidently into this world. This confidence is not about arrogance but rather, assurance of knowing who you are and whose you are.*

We no longer need to live in a prison of loneliness, isolation, and fear to protect our fragile hearts. Instead, we can wear our royal swag and declare the royal edicts over our lives and those we are meant to lead.

What is an edict? Simply put, it is *a proclamation having the force of law*. When a King made an edict in Biblical times, it was irreversible. Town criers would shout the edict in the streets and post the new law at the city gates so everyone could see and hear it. What used to be normal was decreed to change now or face the consequences. Old ways of living were forced to comply with new standards. Disobedience was not tolerated. As a child of the King, He has given us that same authority to set things in motion and order in our life by our decrees! Yes, that means our words. Our words have power! "From the fruit of their mouth, a person's stomach is filled; with the harvest of their lips, they are satisfied. **The tongue has the power of life and death**, and those who love it will eat its fruit" (Proverbs 18:20-21, NIV).

We can see in Genesis that God's words brought everything into existence and order. Because we are made in His image, we've also been given that powerful tool to speak life or death over our lives. We must reject negative thought patterns and critical words that have shaped our current reality and instead choose life by speaking His words of life and truth.

> *Don't let your mouth betray you even when your mind wants to. Know His Word so you can remind yourself of Truth when faced with doubt.*

As a royal princess of the King, embrace each step with confidence and grace, showcasing His stunning handiwork. Let your life become a beautiful echo of His glory here on earth by allowing His strength to empower you to push back darkness and radiate His light so brilliantly that you also will be turning heads everywhere you go!

"For we are God's masterpiece. He has created us anew in Christ Jesus so we can do the good things He planned for us long ago." (Ephesians 2:10, NLT).

My Closing prayer for us:

Heavenly Father, as we close this book, prepare us to live with Your truth echoing in our hearts. Don't let us easily forget what You have revealed. Please help us to become more self-aware and reflective of the things that You have brought to our attention. May we walk in greater truth and freedom and share it with others. Amen.

To the reader

Thank you for taking the time to read this book. I pray you have found encouragement and hope throughout its pages. If you know of someone who might benefit from any of the stories and truths shared throughout, please pass it along to spread the same encouragement and hope to them. Your journey with this book matters to me, and I would be honored to hear how it has inspired or challenged you.

Please contact me at: *thiscinderellahasbigfeet@yahoo.com*
or you can find me at *lynettebeeler.my.canva.site*
I look forward to hearing from you.

www.ingramcontent.com/pod-product-compliance
Lightning Source LLC
Chambersburg PA
CBHW070552050426
42450CB00011B/2822